"I have silently observed a mother walk her path of unwanted grief with tears and courage. The words within this book offer the hope and possibility to be able to move through the loss of a loved one. Through gently guiding her reader to embrace their life's challenges, she illustrates what is possible and how everything you need to live a full life is stored beautifully within you. This book is uplifting and truly inspirational. The message throughout the book is about the healing power of love. The culmination of her words are an amazing tribute to her beautiful daughter Jenna who continues to light the world with her smile."

- Kathryn Davi Cardinale., author,
Joseph, My Son, My Guide

"It took me years to realize that suffering is optional. It's always a choice. This book creates possibility and will empower you to take action. When I was Dena's golf coach, I had the honor of enrolling her in a conversation allowing her to explore new possibilities within herself that would allow her to take new actions and discover different outcomes. As she shares her journey with you throughout this book, you will begin to understand that we are the culmination of our thoughts and we have the power to make our thoughts empowering ones."

- Kim Larsen, Vietnam Veteran,
Golf Coach, Musician

"Having been a longtime friend and inaugural University of San Francisco's golf teammate of Dena's, I am honored to be able to walk our voyage of life together. We share many bonds. Our bond was built through the game of golf knowing that we were not playing against one another. We were playing against ourselves. We were simply playing against the course (life) with the goal to raise our own personal bar, stay in the game, and to keep a positive perspective. To this day, Dena is still a mentor and teammate in the game of life where we have experienced a whole new realm of hazards. I am happy to still have her on my team."

- Jody Banovich, Owner - Parvino Wine Co.,
USF Golf Teammate

"If you are suffering, Dena's heartfelt storytelling will open you to a powerful truth – we are more than our bodies and thoughts. We are pure spiritual energy here to live a life with intention and meaning. Beyond death, her daughter's life purpose continues through Dena as a catalyst for awakening and connection. Together they show the way forward through loss and despair."

- Julia Novak, B.S., LM   Spiritual Counselor,
Psychic, and Energy Healer. www.julianovak.net

you are
STRONGER
than you know
my daughter told me so

*A Mother's Extraordinary Journey of Hope,
Strength & Inspiration After the Tragic Death of
Her 14-Year-Old Daughter*

DENA M DERENALE-BETTI

You Are Stronger Than You Know
My Daughter Told Me So

First Edition

ISBN-13: 978-1542570909

ISBN-10: 1542570905

CreateSpace, Charleston, South Carolina, USA

2017

I dedicate this book to the

power and love that

lies inside each one of us.

In loving memory of my dear daughter

Jenna Betti
(1999-2014)

My Forever Shining Light

Contents

Acknowledgements i

Foreword v

Introduction viii

Chapter 1 1

Chapter 2 30

Chapter 3 44

Chapter 4 61

Chapter 5 76

Chapter 6 90

Chapter 7 108

Chapter 8 120

Chapter 9 148

Acknowledgements

This book is written with special thanks to:

- Paul Betti, I thank you for how you have touched my soul, our deep intimate love, how you have made me a better person, your humor, your parenting, your talents and your devotion to our family. Together, we have been forced to battle and navigate life's greatest heartaches and challenges and it moves me to tears to know that we have strengthened our ties to one another throughout every step of the way. I love you with all my soul. You are a beautiful gift.

- Jenna, Julia and Gigi, I thank your souls for choosing me as your mother. You have given me a depth of love that words cannot describe. I am honored to call each one of you my daughters. You are beautiful souls…giving, kind, ambitious, wondrous souls. I see the beauty of life and the splendor of the human experience in each of you. Like pieces to a puzzle, you complete me. May you always know my love and devotion to you.

- Mom & Dad, I thank you for the amazing roots you have given me. I thank you for pushing me to always be the best me, the strongest me, the most driven me. I thank you for allowing me to witness that life isn't always easy but that giving up isn't an option. I thank you for allowing me to pursue my passions. I thank you for your love and dedication to me, for having beautiful conversations with me and for encouraging me to make the world better. I thank you for holding me up every time I get knocked down. Most of all, I thank you for loving me.

- Sissy, you are not only my sister, you are my soul-sister. I thank you for your unwavering faith in me, for your affection for me and for the person I stand here today to be. I thank you for your kind, sensitive and emotional heart and for showing me life through the emotional lenses of your soul. I thank you for teaching me, guiding me and your love for me. I thank you for walking this spiritual journey with me. You are the yin to my yang.

- Teresa & Lorenzo Betti, I am truly blessed to have you as my mother and father-in-law. There has never been a day when I haven't felt the love and devotion you have to our family and to your grandchildren. I am forever grateful.

- Kristy & Armin, I thank you for our beautiful friendship and the bonds we share. I thank you for your love for me. I thank you for rushing to our side and never leaving us. I thank you for your sister and brotherhood. I thank you for our rich conversations, vacations and all the joy and richness you bring to my life. May you always know how much you mean to me. Kristy…you are the Thelma to my Louise.

- Kathryn Cardinale, I thank you for your counseling and for showing us that grief is necessary and very personal. I thank you for your friendship, for holding me up when I didn't know if I was going to be able to hold myself up and for sharing Joseph's messages with me. I will always consider you a gift from God.

- Amber Cole and Suzy Hammond, I thank you for rushing to our side and for all you did to hold us up and honor Jenna. I thank you for the months you sat around our kitchen table and talked with me. I thank you for co-founding #hersmile Nonprofit with me and the countless hours you devoted to creating an organization built on hope, strength and inspiration.

- Lorraine, Frank, Ezio, Teri, Kim and every member of both Paul and my family, I thank you for rushing to our side, for your love and for your support. For the bonds of family have been strengthened by all that you have given of yourselves. May you always know how much you mean to us.

- Laura Patrick, Michelle Foxworthy, Deneen Wholford, Andy Armosino, Chris Loscalzo, Jackie Hopkins, Rami Muth, Barbara Phelan, Cyndi Silva, Will Tran and every volunteer who has given of their time and heart to make #hersmile Nonprofit the organization it has grown to become, I am honored to work with each and every one of you. You have shown me the great power we possess by coming together, the loving impact we can make and that the richness in life is deeply housed in the contributions we make to one another.

- Michelle Foxworthy, Monica Scodeller, Colleen Gianatiempo, Jody Banovich, Michelle Hamilton, Diane Rivest, Kristy Safarians, Jen Moser, Jeri Bluth and Julia Novak, you are my soul sisters. I thank you for your heart, your spirit, your art, your passion and, mostly, I thank you for being able to live in a space with me beyond what we can see, touch and feel. You have brought such soulful abundance to my life. You each personify grace and your souls decorate this world.

- To our community of friends and neighbors from Martinez, CA, to our neighboring towns, to our DFC Soccer Community, to our local school district, the Pauline's, Jonathan Eagan, Eva King, Mark & Julie Hood and Amie Hair, you have cried with us, you have loved us, you have fed us, you have created keepsakes for us, you have championed #hersmile Nonprofit as your own and you have celebrated Jenna with us. There will never be enough words to express the impact you have made in my life for it is through each and every one of you that I have learned the healing power love has in a person's life. I am eternally grateful. May I live the rest of my days paying forward all you have done for our family.

- To my Knitting Crew from Hillsdale High School Nicole Donegan, Amy Bergstrom, Sharon Estrella, Jamie Lentzner, Kristi Will, Nicole Ryan, Christine Peeso, Lisa Herren, Stephanie Degen, Michelle Zalba, Staci Ross, and Lisa Breitensten thank you for the year-long of gifts you sent to our family. Neither time nor distance stopped you from holding me up with your love. I have always felt deeply blessed to call each and every one of you my friend.

- Kim Larsen, I thank you for coaching me on a scale much greater than how to hit a little white ball into a golf hole. You opened up my mind to a different way of processing the world. You taught me that the opulence of life lies in our ability to be aware of the thoughts that permeate our being. I am forever grateful for your coaching me in the Great Game of Life.

Foreword

Have you ever wondered why life takes you down a path that was completely unforeseen? In many of our lives it's not uncommon for us to experience times that shake our inner core and completely change how we knew life to be. Life can change directions on a dime leaving us completely ill prepared to deal or cope with a horrific tragedy or hardship. In the wake, it is you that is left with the pieces of your life to pick up. How will you cope? Will you ever really be able to move on?

On March 2, 2014, my dear friend Dena, was forced to ask herself these same questions.

I believe the answers to those very difficult questions comes from within. As I witnessed Dena's journey unfold, I learned we all have a choice in how we deal and cope with life's greatest challenges and heartaches. She taught me the power and impact of free will. I witnessed Dena choose a life of contribution despite her circumstances.

Her grief has metamorphosed into the divine calling of providing hope, strength and inspiration to others in times of tragedy and loss. By choosing to give back to others, she's become a channel of hope, grace and peace to all whom she touches. She has brought beauty into her life and has a deeper connection to her soul and higher-being because the power of how she has directed her thoughts and emotions.

This revelation in Dena has transpired an amazing transformation within me. It has ignited my soul. It has filled my being with love and hope. She has chosen to smile despite her pain. As a child my father used to tell me, "Smile, it does not cost you anything but it gives a lot." I now understand the greatest gifts we experience throughout life start from within...a smile, a powerful thought or intention. For it is only through yourself that you can create the positive energy that generates the warm glow that blankets your soul in a time of need, sadness and grief.

Dena chose to live a life of meaning by becoming aware and listening to the thoughts she entertained. She did not use judgement or self-implication. She listened with the intent to understand and then decided to live a life of intention despite her pain.

Dena harnessed the love for her daughter and family in order to move forth towards the light. Only good comes from the light; from pure raw energy. Through moving forward with love as her intention she has been able to help and support not only herself but the world around her. Her book, *You're Stronger Than You Know, My Daughter Told Me So*, will lead you on a path of self-discovery, help you connect with your authentic self and help you become aware of your truth. You will learn the only way to have a full life despite your circumstances is through love and intention.

So, how does one begin to ignite and connect to their soul? I believe the answers are within each and every one of us. As you embark on Dena's journey, you will be stripped from the shackles of your ego, learn to quiet your mind and connect to your soul. For I, too, now understand, we are all stronger than we know. Just listen and trust. I believe we are not responsible to seeking the answers to the "whys" in our lives but we are responsible for seeking the truths in our journey. Dena's story is a story of the power of self-discovery.

Monica Scodeller
Friend & Soul Sister

Introduction

Out on a Walk

I remember March 2, 2014, very well. Jenna, my 14-year-old daughter, had club soccer tryouts in the morning. Paul, my husband, had taken her to practice and afterwards Jenna's younger sisters and I met up with them at my sister-in-law's house for my niece's birthday brunch. It had started out to be a lovely day. After the brunch Jenna and I drove back home together. Paul and the girls stayed a little longer. Jenna had plans to meet up with a friend, so I dropped her off at home to shower, while I ran a couple of quick errands. Jenna texted Paul and me, asking if she could take a walk around our neighborhood with her friend. We agreed, reminding her to be careful. When I arrived home, Jenna had already left.

I headed out for a walk around our neighborhood with our six-month-old Labrador, Pepper. I didn't see Jenna while out on my walk but assumed we had headed out in different directions. As our walk was coming to an end, my cell phone rang. It was Paul. I heard complete terror in his voice. He kept repeating, "I can't believe it! I can't fucking believe it!" He moaned between his words. My heart stopped, and I shrieked back at him, "What…what happened? Paul! Tell me what happened!" Barely able to formulate the words, he screamed, "IT'S JENNA! YOU HAVE TO COME HERE! COME TO THE TRAIN TRACKS! YOU HAVE TO COME NOW!"

My world began to spin. My legs grew weak. My lack of focus took me into the street. "Jenna? What happened to Jenna?" I wailed. "Where are you?"

"Come . . . come to the train tracks!" Paul shrieked.

I lost the words as they entered my being. I began to run. I had forgotten that I had Pepper with me, until I flew over her body and collided with the asphalt. Finding my feet again, I ran, but in a moment like this you feel like you're on a perpetual treadmill, where any sense of distance evades you. Instinctively, I ran home. The front door was wide open. In that moment, the words 'train tracks' rushed to the forefront of my mind. Paul had said, "Come to the train tracks!" The words flooded my mind. I ran up the steps to my front door, pushed Pepper in and slammed the door closed. Again I ran and ran, praying, "Please, dear God, please let her be okay." I was acutely conscious of those pleading words and my gasping breath.

The Cyclone[R] gate that led to the train tracks is a block and a half from my house. Arriving at the site, I saw a distraught crowd gathering. The first person I saw up close was a neighborhood friend. "What happened?" I yelled. She gripped her mouth with the palms of her hands, shaking her head in disbelief, her body language screaming sheer terror as she pointed to the opening in the fence.

I ran through the gate and down a steep embankment. I plunged to the deep auburn lava rocks that flanked the train tracks. I saw paramedics surrounding something about 300 yards over my left shoulder. I ran as fast as I could. My mind went blank. I stopped as I neared the scene. Did I stop because I already knew?

The Ultimate Loss

On that tragic day, my daughter, Jenna, was struck and killed by a service train.

We soon learned that she and her friend had taken the shortcut through the train tracks on their way back home from their walk. They had sat on the tracks to talk and carve out words in the railroad ties. They had both put their cell phones down. An unanticipated train sneakily and instantly descended upon them. Seeing people in the distance, the conductor blared his horns. According to witnesses, each fled to a different side of the tracks. But, Jenna had gone back to grab her phone and the train struck her in the back. That split decision had cost her life and changed our lives forever.

From the second I stood on the train tracks and realized my baby girl was gone forever, my consciousness expanded. I knew I had a huge decision to make. Move on in darkness and live out our days in despair, or I could harness the feelings I have for Jenna and our family and somehow find a way to move on with love in my heart. My reality spun turbulently inside me. Within minutes, I told Paul that this tragedy would not define us, implying that this would not ruin us. I refused to ask why.

That's where my healing journey began. I forced myself to seek understanding about how we could move forward in our lives with intention. The easy route would have been to allow ourselves to be victims, to think that life happened to us, and we had no control over it. I didn't deny the tragedy we'd been dealt. Yet, from all my years of observation, mental training and awareness, I understood that we still had the power to define our reality. People and situations in my life had shown me it was possible. Now my beliefs would be tested. Would I be able to walk the walk?

An Intimate Journey

I have been asked if I ever experienced the Dark Night of the Soul—the feeling that God had abandoned me—as a consequence of Jenna's passing. It's the moment in one's life when nothing seems to make sense, and life seems to be devoid of purpose or meaning. The Dark Night pulls on you to retreat from the world and lie dormant in bed. It beckons jealousy and anger to take up residency in your soul, leaving darkness and despair in its wake.

Something inside me died when Jenna passed away, but it wasn't the sort of death we commonly understand it to be. It wasn't the hopelessness and darkness of the Dark Night. It was the death of my illusory identity. It was the death of how I thought our lives were supposed to play out.

As you embark on reading this book, perhaps you'll travel on a path that is different from your own. You'll take an intimate journey into the strength and power we all share. You will learn how life has been preparing you for your personal circumstances all along, how expanding your consciousness will transform you. And, you'll walk away understanding that what you choose to focus on will shape your future. Finally, it is my hope that I can show you how happiness and growth after trauma are absolutely attainable.

I invite you to accompany me as I share my soul's journey and reveal how our paths—yours and mine—were meant to cross

Chapter 1

What Defines You

Paul and I married in the late 1990s. I felt blessed to have found such an amazing person with whom to spend my life. He has always loved and supported me for the person I am and aspire to be.

Even though I was excited to start the rest of my life with him, I still struggled with the heartache of losing my dad to cancer that year. Dad and I were extremely close. He married his first wife when he was in his early twenties and had three amazing children. Although the marriage ended, he loved his family very much. He used to tell me that he could never love any one of his children any more than the other, joking that he wasn't smart enough to know how to do that. Still, I benefited from his being older when he married my mom and they had me. With age came a greater sense of wisdom and understanding for him. He had been emotionally abused as a child, which left indelible scars. He struggled to manage his anger, jealousy, and sense of self-worth, much of which I witnessed and absorbed as a young child.

I also witnessed my dad never wanting to give up on being a better person, more loving and more forgiving. At times, I struggled to understand how he could be willing to forgive those who had wounded him so deeply. Now, as I've grown older, I've learned that the forgiveness he bestowed upon others was, in reality, a gift he gave to himself. As his awareness about the true essence of life grew, he showered his soul with self-love, despite what life's circumstances and hardships had brought him. Witnessing his life taught me about one's internal struggles and, despite our hardships, to never give up.

We were by dad's side when he died. The hospice worker helped us every step of the way. She explained that it can be difficult for the soul to let go of the physical body, and that it was important for us to let him know that it was okay for him to go, to tell him how much we will always love him, and that we were going to be okay. We did as she said, meaning every word. As I watched him take his last breath, a sense of peace rolled through me. I knew without a doubt that his soul would soar and that the love we shared was one of my life's greatest gifts.

The Circle of Life

I felt called to create life after dad died. There was so much to do, so much life to live, and the moment was now. Witnessing his death made me ever so aware that I was alive and that the true essence of life existed in the giving and receiving of love. I began to understand that it's through love that we discover our life's path and our place in the world. And, it is there that the soul's journey unfolds. We are all here for very powerful reasons, and the lessons and gifts of our lives all unfold at different times and during different seasons. As the journey of life reveals itself, keep love and compassion in your heart as each new door opens or closes. As I focused on the gift my dad was and will always be in my life, a door opened to the next chapter in my life—The Circle of Life.

That next chapter would prove to be a special one. Although Paul and I wanted a family, we had plans to enjoy being newlyweds first. But, after my dad's passing, I felt a strong internal shift. The unwinding path of the Circle of Life washed over me and Jenna was born one month shy of the first anniversary of my father's death. From the moment of her arrival, Paul and I began an amazing love affair with her. She made me feel complete. I felt as if I had known and loved her all along. As I stared into her eyes for the very first time, little did I know that

3

she would help me become a better person and would challenge me in ways I never knew possible.

Jenna's untimely passing has required me to utilize every coping and resiliency tool I have in my toolbox. I have spent a lifetime learning to cope with the world around me, starting as a young child when I began to be aware of the different strategies that appeared to work and not work. Yet, losing Jenna proved to be the ultimate test of understanding what lies within me.

We are All Different Yet the Same

I've spent much of my life exploring why everyone deals with life's challenges differently. As a little girl, I was already somehow able to cope with certain people or situations better than others in my family. And, as I began to look beyond my own family dynamics, I started to understand that we all interpret people, situations and the world around us from our own unique perspective. I found this to be amazing. I realized that I often used different coping tools from the people around me.

Everyone is dealt a different hand in life, including struggles with parental relationships, abuse, trauma, finances, coping with job loss, divorce, illness, or death. The list is endless. Our life's circumstance shapes the people we are and the people we are willing to become.

4

I heard a story once about a researcher who had interviewed two brothers having the same father, an abusive alcoholic. The interviewer privately asked each one the same question, "How did you turn out the way you did?" Both brothers replied separately, "Have you met my father?"

The real catch to this story is that one brother was living a full life surrounded by love and connection, while the other brother was following in his father's footsteps. So, even though our life's circumstance makes a great impact on us, how we react is unique. So, it's no wonder that we all come to life's hardships and heartaches with different coping tools. The vast majority of people experience some level of debilitation when faced with one or more of life's challenges, while a small minority seem to navigate them with grace and purpose. So, where does the difference lie in each of us? Is there a process of healthy human development that can help us thrive despite life's tests? I believe there is.

I've spent a great deal of my life exploring human psychology, what fuels personal happiness, peak performance and the ability to cope, and perhaps most important, what it means to be a soulful being. I've seen what works and what doesn't work in my pursuit of a life of peace, contribution and love. The tragic death of my

5

daughter has been the ultimate test. Although no advanced degree in the world could have prepared me for such a devastating loss, it was the years of keen observation and mental practice that provided me with the resiliency to move forward with a life of rich intention and love.

There are countless individual testimonies worldwide of near-death experiences. They provide evidence of our ongoing existence after death, where the oneness of all things cannot be denied, and there is the realization that love bonds all things together.

As our souls embark on the human journey, our purpose is to recognize who we are, which is love and our oneness with the whole. The illusion of our separateness creates a false self that distinguishes itself from others. It is when we become conscious of this that we can reunite with our divinity and find purpose in all things. Experiencing love amid hardship, pain, anger, abuse, trauma and grief is a paradox. The ultimate challenge is to experience sustaining, unconditional love, despite our circumstances, and to understand that we are something far more than the chapters of our life.

What if you believe that a truly fulfilling life is supposed to have inherent hardships and challenges, because only through tribulations can your soul have the opportunity to grow, shed its attachment to the illusion of its ego-centered self, and create a life of deeper, richer meaning and connection? Do you think you might look at life and its struggles differently?

What Makes You, YOU?

You are comprised and shaped by your values and your core beliefs. They create a map showing where you are willing to devote your time and energy. And, they determine the course of your actions while in your physical form. Is the statement, "Know your values and beliefs and you'll know yourself," really true? The answer is 'yes'—and 'no.' Our core values and beliefs have great power in our lives. They direct us around every turn.

However, as you dive deeper into the depths of who you truly are, you must first recognize that the values and beliefs you entertain day in and day out only shed light on part of the narrative. People are also well-versed in adopting beliefs about themselves and the world around them that are rooted in their peers' influence. For example, if someone believes you are not attractive, it is likely you will believe them and so on. The important message is that you are not the illusion of someone else's perception of you. You are not the sum of your life's circumstances and hardships, either. You are so much more, so much greater.

The first step is to become aware of the values and beliefs you have accepted as your own, but are actually someone else's mental construct. Then, only through conscious awareness can you tap into the power and energy you have within and are authentically yours.

The ensuing true magic is the inner knowing astounding beauty and love from that inner place. It also allows your mind to follow a course of action and connect with the larger intention. Whereas, believing any task is virtually impossible closes off such personal capacities and affects the ultimate outcome of your life.

Not being aware of the thoughts that determine your every action is one of the greatest hurdles you will face, when trying to achieve something. Being able to calm your mind, devoid of chatter, will allow you to become aware of such thoughts and the road map you've created in accordance with your values and beliefs that determine your life's course. True awareness will awaken you from your unconsciousness, propel you into a powerful mindset and transform your life forever. To achieve lasting change in your life—and a rich human experience, despite your circumstances—you must become aware of how you interpret your world and yourself.

Think for a moment. If all people have different values and beliefs, what is the truth? The only truth is that your soul's nature is based on the law of unconditional love. Conversely, when your core values and beliefs are predicated on your life's circumstances and your peers' opinions of you, your true purpose may never have the opportunity to unfold.

Learning to Be Aware

Life's challenges have a distinct way of shaping us. Much of the inner ramifications and ensuing internalized sense of ourselves became deeply embedded in our subconscious at a young age, when we were typically unaware that they were occurring. Still, certain adults can vividly recall a decision they made during their youth that contributed significantly to creating the person they are today. For us to have the life we deserve and are meant to experience, we must first become aware of the thoughts, emotions and beliefs that dictate our every move.

When she was a young girl, my good friend Sarah's sister died at age eight. Their mother was devastated. Her father was angry and drank heavily in hope of masking his pain. Sarah did her best to care for her mother and be a good daughter. As a teenager, she rarely went out so as not to worry her mother. She worked hard to contribute to the family's finances. When her father eventually abandoned her and her mom, Sarah did her best to keep it together, vowing to stay strong despite her own personal pain.

As a young adult, she married a kind man and had children. Still, Sarah struggled to be truly happy. She lacked the awareness to realize that the hardships and trauma she had experienced as a child were still dictating her thoughts. It took her years to realize that she believed she did not deserve happiness. She had spent so long keeping it together and caring for others that she truly had no idea of the belief system that controlled her. As a result, Sarah retreated from her family, no longer wanting the responsibility of caring for everyone else. Her childhood trauma continued to haunt her.

Is it possible to have a joyous life despite its traumas? If so, how? The answer is emphatically yes. The how is by learning to be aware.

I was fortunate to have a level of awareness during my adolescence that proved pivotal. When I was 15 years old, I believed I was wise beyond my years. What teenage girl doesn't believe this at that ripe old age? I challenged my mother with my self-righteous beliefs and asserted my unyielding independence — just as my teenage daughters do with me today. She reacted with sheer annoyance, completely understandable in retrospect. Still, that was the year I drew a line in the sand and made what would be one of the greatest decisions of my life.

On this particular day, I asked my mom why she was so bitter. She replied: "Dena, once you've had life happen to you, you will understand." She wasn't wishing that fate on me. She would never do that. She just meant that life has a way of changing you, hardening you. It was in that moment that I declared silently to myself that I would NEVER let life do that to me. I would never become bitter — no matter how life unfolded. I believed I could have a different outcome.

This is how two children raised in the same family with the exact same parents can have such different experiences. The illusion of our beliefs and decisions can either help or hinder us. I've experienced this with my siblings and witnessed it over and over in other families.

Perhaps you subscribe to Sigmund Freud's school of thought on taking control of what causes you pain or pleasure. Or, Wayne Dyer's approach of tapping into the field of energy around you to create a life of intention. Maybe you adhere to Shawn Achor's concept of capitalizing on happiness to improve performance and maximize your potential. The point is, not one of these teachings can be successfully implemented without your first becoming aware of the thoughts that drive your own behavior. You may have the best intentions to live a fulfilling life despite your circumstance. But, if your inner thoughts and beliefs are otherwise, you can't help but fail. How could someone, like my friend Sarah or myself, ever feel happy if our inner thoughts continued to tell us we didn't deserve to be?

If you can begin to become aware of the daily thoughts and beliefs that you unconsciously invest in, you will gain the ability to discover or reclaim your own powerful reality at any given time — no matter the hardship you are facing. This doesn't mean you won't feel emotional pain ever again, but it does mean that you'll be able to navigate yourself out of pain and towards your intention, with greater ease and purpose.

It takes effort to develop the awareness you'll need to identify from within what makes you tick. The key, once you become aware of the thoughts and beliefs that drive your actions, is to NOT dwell on and judge them. That will only make matters worse. Simply notice that they exist within you and then, with intention, CREATE new beliefs and direction for yourself. Changing beliefs is surprisingly easy. You simply stop believing in your old beliefs and create anew. I bet, like most people, you used to believe in something very strongly but later decided to discard it, because experience showed you otherwise.

It's important to note that you may need to slightly shift your value system in order to alter a core belief. Certain values make it easy to dissolve a core belief, while other values hinder the process.

For example, if I value relationships but believe that only some people are deserving of my affection, I have set myself up for a limited amount of connection in my life. On the other hand, if I value relationships with all people and things on Earth, I then make it possible to believe all people and things are deserving of my care and compassion.

Another example. If I value contentment but believe it to be unattainable should a devastating loss occur in my life, I inherently set myself up for heartache. But, if I value contentment despite life's circumstance, I open the door for the belief that I can find joy, despite life's hardships and heartaches.

Do you see how that works? Knowing the words and framework you honor around your values and beliefs either limits or frees you to have the life your soul came here to experience.

An Individual Sport

Learning to create a new reality may come with its own bag of challenges, but it's entirely worth the effort.

I spent 10 years, from my mid-teens to my mid-20s, playing competitive golf. It's a period in my life that I treasure on many levels. Unfortunately, much of that time I found myself struggling to become the caliber of player I'd dreamt of being. Mentally, I beat myself up for failing to reach the heights I had envisioned. The more I criticized myself, the worse my golf game became, and my mental state continued to deteriorate. It was during my college years at the University of San Francisco that I struggled the most. During that time, I found solace in such subjects as philosophy and sports psychology, because I felt compelled to grab on to anything that could give me a greater competitive advantage. I also had a golf coach who aided my personal development in ways I never imagined at the time.

Kim Larsen was my coach and a free spirit gifted with a life perspective much broader than mine. He had lived in his own personal darkness for many years, having suffered from post-traumatic stress disorder (PTSD) from the time he served in the Vietnam War. He shared with me his personal journey out of darkness. His PTSD would not allow him to stop reliving his horrific past. Becoming aware of the motion picture that constantly played in his mind allowed him, for the first time since his military service, to live in the present moment, where suffering fails to exist. He was able just to be. In the moment, there is no past or future. Our stories literally cease to exist. My coach had begun to understand that he was partially responsible for his suffering, which he had exacerbated by perpetuating thoughts and images he unwittingly allowed to play unchecked in his limbic mind, a pattern that had previously resided in his unconscious. When a mind is conscious of the present moment, devoid of past experiences and future anticipation, the abundance of a fulfilling life can unfold and be shared. In other words, you release the baggage from the moment.

Kim often shared a great quote with me from an unknown author, "Try to change it and it will persist, or become aware of it and it will dissipate."

In his book *The Power of Now,* Eckhart Tolle states, "When you recognize the unconsciousness in you, that which makes the recognition possible is the arising consciousness, is awakening. You cannot fight against the ego and win, just as you cannot fight against darkness. The light of consciousness is all that is necessary. You are that light."

Only through the light of awareness can you create lasting change in your experiences and, on a grander scale, your life. Too many times we want to run from our pain or control a future outcome, when all we need to do is become aware of the thoughts, emotions, and beliefs that occupy our being. Be in the moment. Become aware of your personal monologue.

But how? Kim taught me how to first be aware of my body. I suggest that you start with your own body awareness, as well. It's the easiest place to connect.

He first had me take note of the energy flowing throughout my body, as I took my stance over the golf ball. "Start at your feet. Do your feet feel relaxed? Where is the weight distribution in your feet? Move up to your ankles and then to your knees. Are your knees flexed? Is there tension in the knees, or are they relaxed? Move up to your thighs. Do you feel energy flowing throughout your thighs and up to your buttocks? Move to your hands now. Could you hold a bird in your hands and not let it fly away, but not hold it so tight that you hurt it?" He continued as I scanned the rest of my body with an internal observing eye. "Look at the target now. Look down at the ball. Notice the shape of the dimples and then, one more time, look at the target. What details do you notice as you look out toward your target? Now keep the image of the target in your mind. Take a swing now."

Each time I swung, I would deeply inhale, and then exhale on my down swing. I was becoming aware! I quickly learned that I had blind spots — or lack of awareness — in my golf swing. Only through consciousness can you acknowledge unconsciousness. I was heading in the right direction. When you are aware, there is no inner dialogue about the thing you are observing; there is no judgment or chatter; there is simply awareness. You are making progress.

Not only did my awareness about my golf game begin to grow, but so did every other aspect of my life. Because of my body awareness, I became aware of the thoughts I entertained regarding my golf game. It was no surprise that my thoughts had been self-defeating, considering the results I had been experiencing. It had become a vicious cycle. I began to hear the words I would say to myself: "You put in all this practice, and you still don't shoot under par. If people are telling you what a great swing you have, then why doesn't it work better?" The fact of the matter is our experience reflects exactly what we think, and our mind continues to find evidence to prove that our thoughts are correct.

As my personal awareness grew, first from noticing the energy that moved throughout my body, then to the thoughts I entertained, I began to realize that we all have the internal capacity to live the life our soul was meant to live. This personal awakening shed light on the game at which I had struggled to excel. As I became more aware of the energy flowing throughout my body through daily body awareness exercises, I began to understand that I did not feel called to the game as much as I had convinced myself. My pursuit to be great afforded me many building blocks for the rest of my life, yet I became very clear that playing golf wasn't in alignment with my life's purpose. Pursuits not in alignment with our soul's calling create a sense of heaviness within our body, whereas endeavors in alignment with our higher purpose flow steadily, like calm waters along a meandering stream.

I knew I wanted to get married and have a family. I also wanted my financial world to be secure. Pursuing the life of a professional golfer would make all that I felt called to have in my life very challenging. Clarifying what was important to me arose out of the overall level of awareness in my life and it all started with my desire to hit a little white ball! The amazing thing is that once I became aware, I began to disconnect from my ego. The same can happen for you.

Your ego creates the framework for your identity, defining you by your possessions, your achievements, your reputation, and how you perceive yourself as being different or special as compared to the world around you. It's the part of me that believed I needed to be a great golfer to matter in the world. It falsely defines how you fit in the world. It is also the part that crumbles when an identity shift takes place. It's one with the Dark Night of your soul.

The paradox is that by letting go of the superficial desires of your ego, you're able to harness your connection to the universal energy you are one with and connect to your true purpose in life. Bringing awareness into your life allows you to be conscious of your life's purpose and your higher sense of self. It also allows you to disconnect from the suffering associated with the illusion of who you are. By becoming aware and living in the present moment, you can step outside of your suffering and your life's situation. Your essence is one with the greater whole.

Connecting to the Universal Energy Source

Every event we experience allows us to grow more aware, if only we allow our minds to open up to that practice of being. Awareness is not about judgment.

Awareness is our ability to observe. There is no pain or suffering when you are in the moment, being fully present. Again, our human experience is the manifestation of our thoughts and intentions. Mentally reliving the past or projecting into the future may perpetuate much of your life's suffering.

We all have the ability to be in the moment, to be present and conscious. Several months after Jenna passed away, my neighbor, who is a Buddhist, recommended that I try meditation. She explained that they meditate as part of learning to let go of their attachments and to calm the mind. I agreed that inner peace and calmness were essential for my soul's healing. I also knew I needed to be aware of the pain and darkness residing within me, in order to rebuild and strengthen my own and my family's framework. I knew there was no way I could continue to move forward without this heightened level of awareness.

My dear friend Kristy and I signed up for a 12-week meditation class at a local Buddhist monastery. There was a formality to the class and the teachings were couched in historic customs. The first meditation technique we were taught was called Breath Counting. It was recommended that we sit in the lotus position. Okay, that was impossible for me! I opted for "crisscross applesauce" as I sat atop a wooden box with a square pillow under my bottom. A blanket was draped over my lap to keep me warm. "Now close your eyes. Take three deep breaths in and then out, in and then out," said the abbess, as she rang the bells. "Now breathe in and focus on the tip of your nose. When you breathe out, count your breath …1, 2, 3, 4 … Do not force it. Simply count the length of your breath when you exhale, while still focusing on the tip of your nose." For the first three classes, I fought to stay awake. My mind was calm, but I struggled to maintain awareness. Kristy struggled to turn off the chatter in her mind. The abbess called it "monkey thoughts."

By the fourth class, I was determined not to fall asleep. With every breath, I did my best to focus on the tip of my nose, breath in, and then count my breath on the exhale. I was so thrilled when for the first time I didn't fall asleep in class.

I greatly improved during the course. The best way I can explain meditation is a clearing of chatter, being mindful of one's focal point, having a realization that you are more than the sum of your thoughts, you are connected beyond the "I" of your being, and that you are part of a universal energy. As I clear away the thoughts I entertained, an inner peace washed over me. I began to understand that, if I could know my thoughts, I could manifest thoughts as well.

Stakes in the Ground

Knowing who we are and what we stand for is the effect of a life we have consciously created. However, it is only when we co-create our life with the awareness of our connection to our greatest energy source that we can manifest a life of the highest intention. It's at this point that we can put our stakes in the ground and not have them waiver under life's pressures. No one person is exempt from having their core values and beliefs tested. Big and small challenges are inherent.

Are we confident our core values and beliefs will hold up when tested? How often in life do we judge a person by their actions, only to be faced with the same difficult circumstances in our own lives? From criticizing the boss, to becoming a boss, to judging our parents to becoming a parent, to condemning our politicians, to becoming community leaders, we quickly realize the wavering within our own belief systems. So, what causes belief systems to crumble, when our circumstances change and pressures are applied to our own lives?

When our beliefs are connected to the love and light of the highest energy source, they will never falter. It's such beliefs as righteousness, greed, anger, selfishness, arrogance, and insensitivity that disconnect us from the source of our being, and it's through adhering to these low vibrational beliefs that the human spirit can be truly crippled.

Can you identify someone who allowed his or her belief system to wreak havoc upon themselves? How did their beliefs drive their actions?

The Salon & Your Soul

About a year before Jenna passed away, I had an appointment with Mary, my hair stylist. She had been doing my hair since Jenna was a year old. We had bonded over the loss of my father and the loss of her daughter, 8 years prior. Her daughter would have been my age, but had tragically died in an automobile accident when she was just 23 years old. At first, our losses bonded us to one another, but over the years, I paid more and more attention to how she had been processing the death of her daughter. It was completely contrary to how I had grieved the loss of my father.

As I shared earlier, my father and I shared a special bond. It was thirteen short months from diagnosis of cancer to his death. I was 28, a newlywed, and knew one day we would try to start a family. It would have been easy for me to be angry over his passing, because of all that he and I would miss out on. He would never hold our children, watch them grow. They would miss out on knowing their grandfather, having him at their sports games (he loved sports). He wouldn't be able to give me parenting advice and be there for us to spend time together. Yet, with all the emotional pain associated with his passing, I rooted my belief system in a place of love and gratitude. I asked myself, "How can you be angry with his passing? If you're angry, doesn't it mean that you're not appreciating the gift you were given? Not everyone gets to experience the relationship you had with your dad."

Mary had an underlying thread of anger running through her at all times. Every time I went to see her, she seemed to be on an emotional rollercoaster, experiencing the ups and downs with the people closest to her. She was always angry at someone. She seemed to be continuously embroiled in one of life's dramas. She scorned God and said she couldn't wait to yell at him and tell him, "How dare you take my daughter?" She was devoutly religious.

Mary's reaction to her daughter's death deeply affected me. I prayed that she would one day celebrate the gift her daughter was to her and let go of all her anger and disappointment. I told myself that, if something in life ever tragically happened to me, I would not be as bitter and angry as she was.

On this day, Mary was in a bad place. She was angry with her surviving daughter. Her daughter hadn't spoken to her for more than a year. Mary said it felt like another death. As an observer, I could see how their mother-daughter relationship had deteriorated, through the years of low vibrational energy exchange, rooted as it was in righteousness, arrogance, pain and anger.

I felt so free when I walked out of the salon that day. I drove off deep in thought about how her life's circumstances had so negatively affected her. I needed to talk to someone about the thoughts racing inside me. I called Kristy and said, "I just left my hair appointment and I cannot believe, after so many years that Mary is still so bitter and angry about the death of her daughter. I have to tell you, I honestly think, if something ever happened like that in my life, I know I wouldn't let myself react that way."

Kristy and I continued with our conversation and, as good friends do, she helped me work through my bottled-up frustration. Kristy has since shared with me that she clearly remembers that conversation and thinking at the time, "I hope she really could be that strong if something ever happened to her." I had already begun constructing the building blocks of the person I wanted to be and the life I wanted to have—even if something horrible should ever happen. Creation is an element of awareness.

If you learn nothing else from this book, this is the one thing I hope you will remember.

Looking back on my life, it has given me many chances to mentally prepare, through simple awareness, for any looming circumstance. I paid attention to what worked in people's lives and what didn't work. Little did I know, I was laying the groundwork for a level of consciousness I would desperately need to cope and thrive, despite my daughter's death. The same power lies within you.

What Defines You - A Time and a Season

Your soul chooses to be here on Earth for a reason. In the Bible, Ecclesiastes states: "There is a time for everything and a season for every activity under the heavens" (Chapter 3, Verse 1). There is evidence that, every time your soul comes back to the physical world, you have an opportunity to grow, to choose loving kindness, to exercise free will and grow closer to the light and love of your Creator. The physical world provides us

26

with many challenges like time, space, human emotions, and constant change. It is the reflection looking back at you that allows you to understand and appreciate your true essence.

We struggle to understand the true purpose of our being. We ask questions like, "Why are we here?" and "What's the purpose to all of this?" As energy beings, we hold the power to direct our energy, but before we can do that we must understand the essence of our existence. We cannot direct that which we do not understand exists. As our soul travels through many different experiences, the purpose is for it to gain greater perspective and consciousness of itself beyond the ego's sense of self. As I write these words, I can't help but understand what a difficult concept this is.

Have you ever wanted to be great at something? You set goals and put your heart and soul into getting better? For me, it was golf. I wanted to be great. I worked hard to reach my goals. Seasoned golfers told me to enter tournaments, if I really wanted to get to the next level. So, I did. The first tournament I entered was the City Tournament in San Francisco. Surrounded by a large crowd of spectators, I stood on the first tee at Lincoln Park Golf Course and trembled with fear. My entire sense of self stood atop that grassy knoll. It was my turn on the tee block. As I swung back and came through impact, I suddenly became distinctly aware of my body swinging over the top of the ball and pulling my shot deep left into the street that ran parallel to the fairway. That would cost me a two-stroke penalty. I began to tremble. When you do that in golf, you need to re-tee from where you just hit your last shot. I re-hit and did the exact same thing. I wanted to quit. I was humiliated and embarrassed. I fought back tears. Trembling, I hit another shot and hit it down the fairway.

I took a 10 on that hole. My dad was my caddy. "Are you going to give up now? Are you going to quit?" he said with disappointment in his voice. I wanted to give up, but I didn't. I finished my round that day with a terrible score. After years of conquering different situations just like that one, I began to understand that I was not my golf game. I was so much more than my human experience. I began to gain greater perspective and consciousness of an existence that was more than my sense of *self*. I am a loving being and nothing in my human experience would change that, as long as I honored my true essence.

Each stage in life allows your soul to understand its essence and learn how to direct its energy. As you do this, you learn to fuel your own creation. To "know thyself" is the highest form of knowledge. At the heart of self-knowledge is your understanding that you are one with your Creator. You are unconditional love. You are more than your ego, you are your 'self.' I began to understand that I was more than the outcome of my efforts. To be in harmony, your energy must be in balance. The only way to do that is to come to the self-realization that you are, first, energy, and from that awareness to understand that you have the say how that energy is used and directed.

Chapter 2

Jesus, Take the Wheel

I remember when I first realized the depths of my spirituality. When I was 18, a sarcastic, witty, and extremely intelligent college science teacher taught us about the frequency spectrum. He proclaimed that we were all crazy, if we didn't think there was more to this world than what we could see, touch and smell. "You can't see radio waves, yet you can listen to the radio. You can't touch a rainbow, but you can see it. You can't see the Earth rotate, yet it does," he said. The understanding that there was more to the world than what meets our senses would continue to resonate and amaze me.

On the evening of the second day after Jenna's passing, I lay in bed trying to fall asleep. The room was dark, and Paul and I were silent. The day had been long, with many visitors coming by the house to pay their respects. My eyes were weighted closed by heartbreak and exhaustion. My hands postured in a praying position over my sternum. I prayed to Jenna, urging her to go to the light and love of our creator. I prayed that she would continue to do what her soul was intended to do and always remember the enormity of the love for her that we would carry within our souls forever. As I continued my silent monologue, I felt someone press firmly into my left thigh. It startled me. I quickly opened my eyes and gasped. I was staring into the darkness. I had anticipated seeing one of my daughters, but no one was there. I closed my eyes again and prayed: "Jenna...that was scary, but only because this is new to me. I love you and want you to know you can come to me anytime."

The next evening when I lay down to sleep, I prayed again to Jenna. I prayed, urging her to go to the light and love of our creator, our divine and highest energy source. I expressed my unwavering love to her. Depleted, I fell into a deep sleep. I was jarred awake around 3:00 a.m. I opened my eyes. Over my left shoulder, I saw Jenna in a full translucent image of herself. She was dressed in white. Her golden hair flowed as if a fan blew lightly toward her face. A white light illuminated the perimeter of her entire being. She was magnificent. Yet again I gasped out loud and closed my eyes. "Oh, Jenna, Mommy loves you so much. I'm just not used to this. I am so grateful you have come to us. We miss you so much. We love you with all our hearts and souls. I pray you show us the way." I opened my eyes ever so slightly; she was gone.

Even though I longed to feel and see Jenna, seeing and feeling her in spirit was completely foreign to me. I quickly told myself to let go of the fear and be open to a world I couldn't see, touch or smell. Since Jenna's passing, her spirit has gifted us with countless visits. They are powerful and moving. Our willingness to be aware and open has allowed us to receive many precious gifts.

A Gift Through a Picture

Ezio is my husband's cousin. He grew up in Ohio, while Paul grew up in San Francisco. They grew close as teenagers, spending several summers together while visiting their grandparents in Northern Italy. To this day, they are separated by thousands of miles, but the kinship they share transcends time or distance.

When Ezio heard the news of Jenna's passing, he and his wife, Teri, dropped everything to fly cross-country to be by our side. Their visit was a huge surprise. Paul and I wept over their kindness and love for us.

Shortly after their arrival, Gigi, our youngest daughter, snapped a picture of Paul and Teri as they talked to one another outside our kitchen. What Gigi captured on that picture was another miraculous gift.

Picture taken on March 5, 2014 by Gigi Betti

We witnessed a luminescent glow. A full heart rested over Paul's left arm. There were rays shooting from its perimeter. There's a silhouette of a person's face that radiates off to the right side of the photo as well.

I instantly understood the message. It was one of love for those who had given all of themselves to be with us during our darkest and most devastating days. Perhaps it was all about love. Love will carry you through. Let it in and one day you will take flight again. To this day, that picture is an amazing sign of hope.

Thursday Night Mass

Jenna's Mass was held at Christ the King Church in Pleasant Hill, California. Paul and I greeted everyone as they came up to pay their respects to our family. We embraced, locked eyes, and our souls connected. Jenna's casket was open. Despite her being hit by the train, her full beauty lay intact.

The church filled beyond capacity. Again, we witnessed a powerful love. It was important for my soul to speak out loud. As I stood in front of the most loving community I had ever been with, my words birthed from deep within me. I let go — and Jesus took the wheel:

Before I get started, I must first speak to my beautiful daughters Julia and Gigi. It's so important for me to tell you that what I'm about to share with everyone about your sister Jenna does not take away from the enormity of love I have for each of you. I have always told you that Mommy could never love one of you more than the other, and I mean that with every ounce of my being. Please walk this journey of life knowing how very special each of you is. And, I pray that you understand that everyone has their own special journey to travel in

34

this life. I love you both so very, very much, and I will always be here for you...always. Jenna is your guardian angel now. She always had your back and that will never change!

Now, I would like to share with you my warm memories of Jenna. She was born Nov. 19, 1999. It was the last odd numbered date for the next thousand years. She was destined to be something special. As the nurse put her in my arms for the very first time, she started to cry. I looked into her beautiful eyes and told her, "Don't cry, baby, . . . we love you," and that was the beginning of my love affair with this child who was bestowed upon us. She was beautiful from day one.

As she began to grow, we would rock her to sleep and sing her made-up lullabies. Naptime was never easy for her. Paul would put her in the car and drive around for miles until she fell asleep, or he would sit with her if she woke in the middle of the night and watch *Toy Story* in our room until her eyes grew heavy and she went to sleep again. He was so devoted to her well-being. If you only knew how many times he watched *Toy Story* with her. To this day, Woody sits on her bed to comfort her.

Her first formal word was "Hi" at 10 months and she was amazing at the "Hi"/ hand wave combo. She was early to talk and early to walk. She had the most amazing imagination and was the type of child who could play with her toys and talk by herself for hours.

She was blessed to have her Nonni and Nonno watch her twice a week and from the beginning they bonded with her. She loved them with all her heart and soul.

Around one-to-two years old, she scared us more than you could know. Jenna, if hurt or upset, would hold her breath as she cried. She was so strong willed that the breath holding threw off the synapses in her brain and thrust her into a seizure state. One of the first times it happened was with my father-in-law. He tried to clean her nose and as she began to cry and hold her breath, her eyes rolled back. she appeared to be dying in his arms. My mother-in-law called me and told me Jenna was dying. Now, I look back and wonder if it was preparation for what was to come. It happened several times again. Once we had her airlifted from Tahoe to Reno because we thought, again, we were losing her. After seeing a specialist that my sister-in-law had found for us, we were reassured that she was okay and would grow out of this. The doctor instructed us NOT to react the next time she did this…. and to just reassure Jenna that she'd be okay. Do you know how much strength it takes to not react when your child is in need? Again, was this our preparation?

As the years went on she became a big sister, not once but twice. She would sit for hours playing with

Julia. They created the scripts for their imaginary world. They played with their Barbies, paper dolls, and Polley Pockets. You've never seen anything more beautiful than watching them all play together. She was an amazing big sister from the start.

She flourished at preschool and created lifetime friends. At times, it felt like we were going to a different birthday party every weekend. When I dropped her off at preschool, she would cling to me and wrap her arms around my leg. I jokingly called her 'Velcro.' How I cherish those sweet memories now.

Anyone who knows Paul knows his passion for soccer. He couldn't wait for the day to coach her. She was four years old when they started together. Right out of the gate, Paul guided her and helped her to be the player she grew to be. I believe we got our seven goldfish and countless dolls from his bribing her to get goals. One of my fondest memories of her playing soccer in the beginning years was when our team was up more than six goals, and in AYSO there's a no-slaughter rule. Paul sent Jenna back to defense. She was so upset that he was moving her to the back. She thought it was a punishment. I was the center referee. So, to the defense she went, but just to sit down on the field! I was so upset with her. I and told her to get up. She would NOT. I told her if she didn't get up, I was taking the computer away from her for a month. Still she did not budge, but that was my daughter's amazing will.

Then, to elementary school she went. She made a lot of friends, and all her teachers appreciated her. In third grade, Mrs. Travis assigned her to write a story about what she wanted to be when she grew up. She wrote about how she wanted to be a hairdresser and name her salon Jenna Bows. Jenna Bow was my nickname for her. Don't be mad, Jenna, that everyone knows your nickname now. She never wanted me to call her that in front of her friends.

As she grew up and blossomed, she cherished her many close relationships. Everywhere she went she made close friends. You could never be just a casual friend of Jenna's. If she liked you, she loved you and was devoted to you. From the soccer field, to catechism, to school, the strings to her heart grew.

I cherish the sounds of her hitting the soccer ball off my bedroom window. Paul would tell her, "I don't care if you break the window . . . break it!" She had power in her kicks and power in her soul, but she was kind-hearted just the same. She was so generous with her sisters. Often, they borrowed her clothes and she never complained. She loved to give them advice. She'd tell them how beautiful they were. She loved Julia's eyes and told Gigi how adorable she was.

Her middle school years formalized her beautiful smile with the removal of her braces. Seventh grade was rocky for us as she exerted her independence. She was beyond her years in so many ways and wanted to grow up so quickly. Paul and I didn't want her out all the time. If it was up to her, she would have been with her friends every day of the week. We negotiated sleepovers, and she never seemed to understand why she was made to turn her phone in during the week. She paid us $20 a month for the data plan for her phone. We were the ONLY parents in the world to make a child do such a thing. We just wanted to teach her responsibility and that everything in life comes at a price.

Eighth grade showed us a young girl who was maturing. She was concerned about what she would do when she grew up, because she wasn't sure yet. She was excited to drive and would ask us if we would take her driving. She didn't want to wait for a thing. She dreamed of high school, formal dances, and all the opportunities yet to come.

In the last four days, I am clear about why she was brought to us. She loved so deeply. From Nonni to Nonno, her sisters, her aunts and uncle, everyone in her family, her friends, her teammates, to her boyfriend, she loved with every ounce of her soul.

Yesterday, Kate Wohlford so bravely came to speak with me. With such courage, she shared this story with me. She and Jenna had second period together. Several months back, they were assigned to watch Zach Sobiech, a 17-year-old boy with terminal cancer, whose last months were chronicled on a YouTube video. The video ended and the two of them were in tears. They questioned why people die young. Jenna told Kate that she believed everybody is put onto this Earth to learn to live life, love, and be a true kind of happy. Once you've learned how to do those things and you are those things, you can leave, because you've mastered what we're all here to do. Kate wrote in her letter to Jenna. "You, Jenna Caprice Betti, had learned how to live life to the fullest, love to the fullest, and be happy to the fullest, which is why you're no longer here with us. You've moved on to do greater things. More than you could have done here. And dear Lord, Jenna, we should've all known that you weren't going to go out quietly. You were determined to make an imprint and oh boy did you. You were a firecracker. A crazy, uncontainable, beautiful firecracker, whose spark will burn in our hearts and memory for a lifetime." Thank you for these words, Kate . . . so profound . . . and so true.

In closing and on behalf of my entire family, words cannot express our gratitude. You have lifted us from darkness, devastation and despair. You have filled our hearts and our home with love, and you have united a community. I will pay this generosity forward and vow not to let this tragedy define our family or our future. We have so much to live for and so much to give. May my dear Jenna rest in peace and fill your hearts. Pray to her often, talk to her, and keep her near for that is where she always wanted to be.

Thank you to our family and closest friends for all you have done for us. On behalf of Paul and me, we love you all so much and will be forever grateful.

From the podium, I was able to honor my daughter, our family, our friends and our community without shedding a tear. The fact that I didn't cry was a miracle. I felt a power fill me, coming from a space I wasn't aware existed. As parents, we've all told our children to be tough and have tried to give them the support they needed to form that inner strength that's so vital to life. Standing amongst all who came to support us, I prayed to Jenna and told her it was now Mommy's turn to walk-the-walk. I prayed that my love for her and our family would give me the strength I needed to speak from my soul. I needed to show our girls that they were going to be okay and that, if Mommy could do it, they were going to be able to do it, too. At that moment, my understanding of the power of one's mindset and the power of love were reaffirmed.

Grace under Pressure

We decided to go to Gigi's soccer game about a week after Jenna passed away. The day was warm and I sat in the car while her team warmed up for their game. I closed my eyes and again prayed to Jenna. Tears rolled down my cheeks as I spoke to her. This time I asked her to help me understand. "Please show me how to move forward with love in my heart." Then the most amazing thing happened, the word 'Grace' flashed on the inside of my forehead as if it were a running credit at the end of a motion picture, and the audio was in Dolby Stereo®. Again, I opened my eyes and confirmed I was alone. I quickly Googled the word 'Grace' and found that it means to honor or favor; to give beauty, elegance, or charm to. I prayed to Jenna and told her I would do my best to carry forward with Grace.

You are Never Alone

For most of us, we would never consider giving our power to someone other than ourselves. In our society, independence, skepticism and critical thinking are encouraged. Yet in the days, weeks and months that followed Jenna's passing, I allowed myself to let go of my pride. I held on for dear life to every ounce of love that was given to us. It is only through unconditional love that the human spirit can endure the harshest of circumstances. Through the giving and receiving of love, you are never truly alone.

Chapter 3

Energy (Awareness)

You've heard the saying, "Life can change on a dime." I've witnessed the truth of that expression. As the days after Jenna's passing marched forward, I found myself recalling that she was just here, I had just talked to her and had just touched her. She was here and now she wasn't. In her place, however, was an eternal continuum of love. I was keenly aware that the love never ceased to exist and, like energy, it only changed forms. Love in its purest state, unconditional love, knows no opposite. It just 'is.' Not only was I flooded with true love from our family, friends and community, I felt it from Jenna — even with her passing.

Jenna and our family have given me an opportunity to have a deeper understanding and connection with my soul and the higher power energy that exists all around us and within us. We all are energy. How we direct and manage that energy is up to each individual. It is up to

YOU. And ultimately it determines our level of happiness and the impact we make on the world around us.

I understand that our physical bodies are form infused with energy. I needed to use my energy to move forward in a way that wasn't destructive. Love is the most powerful emotional energy in the human experience. For many months after Jenna's passing, it was the love and energy of others that kept us moving forward and away from our devastation. As I've shared several times in this book, love in its purest form is unconditional. This isn't the type of love we strive to find, create and keep throughout our human experience. This is the love of our Creator. It is pure. It's not the love whose opposite is fear, hate, disdain, cruelty and darkness. It's the type of pure love a mother feels when she holds her baby. It's the love you feel when you give of yourself, expecting nothing in return. It's the love you feel when you're compassionate toward others.

From the beginning, I understood that although Jenna was no longer physically with us, our love for her was still alive. I sought to allow my love for my daughter to carry us forward. Creating and harnessing a powerful positive reality is one of life's greatest challenges, but I moved forward with awareness that it was possible, as was the fortitude to make it our reality.

Surprisingly, I remember many details from the days after Jenna's passing. One of my most powerful memories is how our family, friends, my daughters' friends, and our community would not let us fall. They held us up with the most powerful love. It was a type of love I had never experienced, nor did I know it existed. You love your children, you love your family, but this love was of a higher wavelength. There was a oneness to it. It spoke to me and changed my awareness of life. Jenna's passing and her subsequent steadfast love changed me forever.

Ocean View

We met Kathryn a week after Jenna's passing. She was the grandmother of one of Jenna's best friends. She did grief counseling as part of her missionary work through the Catholic Church. She truly embodies love. She shared with us that she generally did not reach out to families until three weeks after their loved one's passing. In this case, she felt compelled to be with our family sooner. I am forever grateful that she came to our aid so quickly.

We visited with one another on a regular basis. During one of our visits, Kathryn asked me if I'd be interested in doing a relaxation therapy session with her the next time we met. Since it sounded like it would be beneficial and calming to the pain residing within me, I needed to try it at least. I wanted to do everything I could to lift myself from the depths of grief.

The day of the relaxation session was a beautiful clear morning, and I looked forward to Kathryn's arrival. I knew I needed her help. I longed for peace, even though I knew I couldn't rush myself to attain it. Upon her arrival, we hugged and she asked me how I was doing. I answered with my patent line to anyone who asked that question, "I'm hanging in there." But Kathryn is special. She sees beyond my words, into my soul. She knew the depths of my words. I was literally hanging on for dear life and fighting hard to find my way.

She said I needed to lie on a comfortable flat surface. I suggested my bed. It's a quiet space and we agreed it would work perfectly. She invited me to get comfortable and put a blanket over myself. I did as she directed. I lay down, propped the pillow under my head and pulled the covers over me. I was comfortable. Kathryn directed me to close my eyes throughout the relaxation and to listen to her guided words. "Take a deep breath in and then slowly exhale out," she said. "Again, in . . . and slowly out."

She directed me to focus on my toes, "Wiggle your toes and feel all the stress in your toes leave your body now." With each breath, my body began to relax. "Now move up to your legs. Let go of the stress that fills them. With each breath, you feel the stress leave your body." She moved through each major part of my body. By the time we reached the top of my head, I was only aware of Kathryn's voice. It calmed me and I felt detached from my own reality. The stress I had been holding on to began to dissipate.

"Now, as you let all the stress slip out of your mind and body, I want you to walk over to a beautiful descending staircase. This is your staircase. You can design it as you see fit," she said. "Is your handrail wood, iron, or another material? What are your steps made from, wood, marble or, perhaps, stone? Does your staircase bend or is it straight?" My cerebral cortex began to dance. My staircase had an ornate brushed black, wrought iron handrail with a filigreed flower design, the steps were made of the most beautiful Stratuario Italian marble and the staircase had the most stunning *Gone with the Wind* like curvature to it. "Take a deep breath. With each breath, you will walk down a step . . . one . . . two . . . three," Kathryn guided me all the way down to the tenth step.

I walked down the steps, descending to a place of serenity and pure beauty. "At the bottom, I'd like you to go to the most beautiful place you've ever been. This is your special place," she whispered. The place arose quickly in my mind. I had a great ability for recall.

I'm in Oahu at the Kaneohe Klipper Golf Course. I'm standing on the 13th hole that has an unobstructed, panoramic view of the vast Pacific Ocean. The wind is mild and the sky is a sapphire blue. I look out to the horizon and see the most unbelievable sight, a pod of whales. Their movement is poetic.

"Now take a deep breath," she continued. "Invite anyone you like into your space." I did not hesitate.

"Dad," I say, "will you please come visit me. I miss you so much. I need you. How can I deal with this loss without you?" As I look back toward the tee block, I see him come toward me. He wears the same tan color Dockers and golf shirt he wore while still alive. His full head of silver hair still resembles Dean Martin's classic style.

"Now you may invite whomever else you'd like to your special place," Kathryn instructed.

But before I can formulate my invitation, my dad is one step ahead of me. He leads me to the most brilliant shining white light. It lacks human form, but it is his height, and it glimmers rays of light around its entire perimeter. Love, that's all I feel. I am immersed in an overflowing feeling of love.

Kathryn was quiet now, and I continued to lie silent.

As the light grows closer, Jenna's face comes into focus. I see her golden locks flowing around her face, perfect sun-kissed skin, her beautiful hazel eyes, her eyebrows, her rosy cheeks, her adorable nose, and her amazing smile. We are together again—at last. I speak to her telepathically, pleading these unspoken words, "I miss you so much. I don't understand why you had to go. Please, help me understand. Please, show me what this means. Jenna, this has to mean something." She looks into my eyes. There is so much love, so much understanding. She comforts me and holds me up.

Kathryn spoke, "It's time to say good-bye. Start walking back to your staircase."

My dad guides Jenna, who reverts to the most glorious light I have ever seen, and walks back

toward where they came from. In a flash, they are
gone.

"10 . . . 9 . . . 8 . . . continue to breathe in and out,"
Kathryn added. Once I reached the top of my staircase,
Kathryn said I could open my eyes when I was ready. But
I couldn't open my eyes. I didn't want to leave my dad
and Jenna.

"Please . . . come back . . . . Please!" I silently
pleaded. I was keenly aware of Kathryn waiting for
me to open my eyes.

"Are you okay, honey?" she said, concerned. "Were
you able to visit with anyone?"

I opened my eyes and began to sob.

That day I reconfirmed how terribly difficult it is to
say goodbye. But perhaps my greatest takeaway is that
even though I can't see my dad or Jenna, they are with
me. Even though they feel so far away, they are ever so
near. It's in the quiet of our minds that our souls dance.
In each and every one of us is a purpose, a reason why
we are here. Now I look for stillness and peace in my
mind, so I can experience the true depths of our love and
purpose. It's through love that all is possible.

What is Relaxation Therapy?

Relaxation therapy, or mindfulness exercises, is a therapeutic approach used to teach individuals to center themselves. It helps decrease stress and anxiety for people challenged by a variety of mental disturbances. There is minimal risk involved. In the article, "Is Mindfulness Making Us Ill," author Dawn Foster wrote, "In their recent book, The Buddha Pill, psychologists Miguel Farias and Catherine Wikholm voice concern about the lack of research into the adverse effects of meditation and the 'dark side' of mindfulness." Some people have attributed future breakdowns to mindfulness exercises and believe a drawback of using relaxation therapy is its ability to bring you to a heightened level of awareness of what's causing their stress and/or anxiety. I disagree that this is a drawback. In my experience, this is the goal. However, I want to clarify that becoming aware is distinctly different from a person stirring up hurt feelings or traumas and giving additional fuel to those difficult experiences in the present by judging them or creating conversation around them. The distinct difference is that, in awareness the person notices the thoughts, feelings and emotions that exist within them, devoid of judgment. They simply observe. However, when one notices the recurrence of the same thoughts, feelings and emotions and gives them additional fuel by asking disempowering questions like 'why' and going over them again and again in their mind. One experience observes what exists; the other plays a leading role in the screenplay. Please keep this distinction in mind. It is an important one.

http://www.theguardian.com/lifeandstyle/2016/jan/23/is-mindfulness-making-us-ill.

When an individual is one with the energy flowing through their body, that awareness opens the door for pain, grief, sadness and depression to dissipate. I promise you, it is impossible to perpetuate any of these emotions, if you become aware of the energy those emotions represent within you—their existence and how they flow throughout your body, devoid of judgment and blame.

Six months after Jenna passed away, I began not sleeping well. I would fall asleep, only to wake up at midnight and then again around 3:00 a.m. I found it difficult to fall back to sleep. Not being one to ever have a challenge sleeping, I couldn't understand why this was now becoming an issue. I tried many different things to regain my good sleeping habits. For five weeks, I changed my diet. I replaced our mattress. Still, I was tired during the day and lacked my normal level of productivity. I prayed to Jenna and to the love and light of our Creator for direction.

One evening as I lay down to sleep, I prayed to Jenna, expressed my love to her and asked her to help me regain the restful sleep I so needed and desired. I began to take deep breaths in and out. I focused only on my breath and counted my breath as I exhaled. Again, I breathed in and out. In a flash, I saw my relaxation therapy experience with Kathryn in my mind. It was spirit coming through with the direction I requested. I reset my intention and began that very moment to practice the relaxation technique on myself. I directed myself to focus on my toes, "Wiggle your toes. What energy do you feel? Notice it now." With each breath, my body began to relax. "Now move up to your legs. Do you feel energy flowing through your legs? Is there a stoppage of energy? Notice it now."

I moved through each major part of my body. When I reached my lungs and heart, I again asked myself to notice the energy flowing throughout that region. These areas felt sharply different. There was a pressure similar to what you experience when you hold your breath. I did not try to push it away. I simply began to pay attention to it. I continued to take deep breaths in and out. I instructed myself to do no more than just be aware of the tightness and pressure. I could sense the perimeter of the energy mass. As my focus continued to be present with this particular area of my body, I noticed a great energy release start to take place and the most loving feeling washed over my entire being. I continued on to the rest of my body. When I reached the top of my head, I connected my energy to our one source of being, our Creator. That evening, I fell into the deepest sleep I had experienced in more than six weeks. I slept through the entire night and felt renewed in the morning.

The Bible's Gospel of Matthew states: "Ask, and it will be given to you; seek, and you will find; knock, and it will be opened to you. For everyone who asks receives, and he who seeks finds, and to him who knocks it will be opened" (Chapter 7, Verses 7-8). That night, I asked for spirit to help me. I surrendered the impulse to figure it out or fix it. I listened and became aware and spirit guided me toward a beautiful awakening from within.

Chakras

Prior to this experience, I had little formal training about chakras, the seven major energy centers that radiate throughout your body. From a scientific perspective, I understood that energy either involuntarily or voluntarily runs throughout our anatomy. However, the energy blockage and subsequent release of pure love I felt the evening before was beyond what I had previously experienced.

Chakras — which author Anodea Judith calls "wheels of life" — transform the energy that passes through our body. The blockage of energy I had felt was located at the heart chakra.

Not surprisingly, the heart chakra radiates unconditional love and is located in your chest. It is the locus for encountering challenges with love, grief, and our ability to heal. It is also the balancing point between body and spirit.

My inability to sleep was caused by my lack of connection to my spirit, and thus I had been wrestling with how to come to terms with my love and grief. My body was speaking to me. Simply by being aware of the energy flow, I was able to connect with the healing center of my entire system. Through awareness came dissipation, and I began to process my grief and love in a powerful and alternative way. This energy awareness is available at any moment to free us from our limits, grief and heartaches.

Healing Other's Hearts

Love is the ultimate healing force. It allows us to recognize that we are part of something larger, that we are interconnected with all of life, and we understand that we are one with our Creator. The essence of the human experience is living life from this energy center of love. When the heart chakra is open and the energy can flow freely, not only are we more loving to others, but we are also more loving to ourselves. Love is the most fundamental part of our being. Unconditional love, in its purest form, knows no opposite and transcends any connection to our ego or sense of self.

It means living our life with love and compassion toward others. It means that our heart is open, and we inspire the same in others. It is the root to a feeling of happiness and contentment. Others can feel our love and warmth. They feel loved and accepted unconditionally. People feel at peace around us, as there is no judgment on our part. When we dwell in a space of love toward every experience, we reach to the deepest place that connects us with our true essence, our spirit, our soul. This is the space where our broken heart will begin to mend.

You may be thinking this all sounds idealistic—always living in a space of love and meaning. Believe me, I understand. Once I started venturing away from the sanctity of my home and taking baby steps to becoming social again, time and again I found myself completely drained from the experience. I no longer could relate to the insignificance of it all. I no longer cared to hear about who did what or why the way they did something was the right way. I struggled to find meaning in the mundane. Then, there are the terrible things that happen in the world every day. How could I suggest that a person turn their cheek and deny the darkness that surrounds them in this world? How could I suggest that they would ever feel whole again, if something were taken from them as it had been from us? How could I propose that they forgive, if they've been mistreated? How could there be a God, when there is so much pain and suffering in the world? These are profound questions that most of humanity grapples with. I'd be dishonest if I said I haven't struggled with them as well.

Do you believe that the way you interpret the events of your life and the world around you have a direct impact on what you manifest in your own life? Do you believe in empowering or disempowering beliefs? Are you aware of the beliefs that drive your actions? Do you believe the beauty and love you perceive in the world starts with you — despite what is going on around you? Finally, do you understand the true essence of your being?

Why do some people create meaning despite their life's debilitating circumstances, while others fail to find meaning at all?

Man's Search for Meaning by Viktor Frankl is one of the most beautiful stories about the human spirit that I have read. Frankl describes his experience of being imprisoned for three years in Nazi concentration camps. It led him to discover the importance of finding meaning in all forms of existence, even the most brutal ones. This sense of meaning enables people to overcome painful experiences. Had Frankl not been aware of how he was processing his internment, any ensuing intention toward living with a sense of purpose or meaning would most likely have been lost.

Given the harmful influence of ego-driven judgments, searching for meaning without an underlying foundation of unconditional love can prove futile. To manifest and remember the unconditional love from which you are created, you must first become aware of the energy of thought and movement that runs throughout your body and mind. The way to do that is to be present, conscious and in the moment. Notice your breath, scan your body and notice your thoughts. Being conscious is to be without judgment. Through awareness, you will naturally disassociate from thought.

I do not suggest that you deny life's harsh realities. I suggest that you become aware of how you internalize them. Notice how they make you feel and what meaning you extract from them. Do not judge; simply notice.

It is through our spiritual progression that we understand that we become the mirror of what resides within us. Strip away ego and ask, "Who am I?" Void of ego, which embodies our thinking, feeling and ability to distinguish ourselves from others, the answer is, "I am." We are one with the light and love of our Creator, the highest energy source. In our purest form, we are unconditional love. When we commit to becoming aware of that which we are, everything of beauty and love will manifest from within us. It is at this point that our lives truly have meaning.

Chapter 4

Living a Life of Meaning

When a person experiences loss, it is common to struggle to find its meaning. We often ask disempowering questions: "Why did this happen? What did I do to deserve this? Why did God need my child more than I needed her?" or "Why me?" — only to reply with false and often crippling answers.

Thoughtful Questions

It is extremely important to understand that every human obstacle or hardship has an opportunity or a gift built into it. Again, we must start with awareness. As I worked through my grief over the loss of Jenna, I was attuned to how much love I had for her. Through this inner knowing and as my reality began to unfold, it did not make sense to spend all my energy in darkness and despair. These states of mind were the polar opposite of

61

how I felt about my daughter. I love her. I will always love her.

Without the physical presence of Jenna in our lives, I asked myself powerful directive questions: "What am I going to do with all the love I have for Jenna? How can I project my love for her and my family out into the world? How am I going to react in a way that is uplifting? How can I become better and not bitter?" I reminded myself that we have two amazing younger children. I have a happy marriage. How was I going to move forward and have these relationships flourish despite our circumstances? The probing questions we ask ourselves determine where the focus of our thoughts will be, and thoughts are precursors to action.

As I watched a crew of paramedics work on Jenna, I became highly aware of the two distinct paths I could take. Metaphorically, they were like the railroad tracks laid out alongside her. Neither path was a place I had traveled before. I derived inspiration from Albert Einstein, who once said, "A person starts to live when he can live outside himself."

I recall making the clear decision that I wanted to be the example for our family. But how did I make that decision? In a split second, when I asked myself, "How can I not let this define us?"

So often in life, we look for other people to be the example, when all along we have the power lying deep within us. By asking yourself insightful questions, you can discover that dormant power that resides in your soul. I knew that my husband and I would have to prepare to lead by example, if we were ever going to survive the hardest thing a relationship can endure. I asked myself right then and there if I could dig deep enough, if I could do this, if I could be strong enough, and if I could not only inspire myself, but those around me? Could I allow myself not to be a victim?

When broken open, we are stripped of the identity we once knew. When we experience the ultimate loss and are able to start asking ourselves empowering questions, a universal, internal shift happens. The answers to these questions will begin to manifest themselves into *your* world. Seek and you shall find. Everything that's necessary to answer your questions seems to emerge without effort.

Playing the Victim

People want to figure out the reason for everything they encounter. Asking why, when it comes to scientific findings or inventions, can lead to amazing life-changing discoveries. These new understandings have the capacity to add richness to our everyday experience, if we use them with respect and consideration for all mankind. However, asking why when a tragedy strikes, such as, "Why me? Why our family? Why take my child?" These questions can only lead to personal darkness.

Based on much of the mental and metaphysical exercises I practiced in my early 20s for the benefit of my golf game, I knew asking why had the potential to ruin me and, as a result, my family. Asking why often leads down a path of disparaging conclusions that can sound something like this:

Dena: "Why, dear Lord, did you take our daughter, our beautiful Jenna? I didn't deserve this. I've been a good and honest person."

The Lord does not answer so I answer my own question.

Dena: "Because you're an awful person. You should have been better, done more. You should have never let her take a walk. You failed to protect your child."

As the list of false justifications ensued, I would continue to search for reasons that might explain why I deserved to experience such a horrific loss.

Such questions force you into the role of victim. They become a way of coping with grief and loss through self-justification. It's the stance people take when they believe that life is happening *to* them. However, life just happens. It feels personal at times, but it is not. Circumstances and experiences are changing every moment. Some changes we cause and some we do not, but rest assured that it's impossible to get through life without undergoing change.

The Wheels of Change

How many times have you heard a friend or family member say, "I hate change," or "I like to be in control." Ironically, Jenna told me many times that she hated change. When she was a baby, she cried for a week straight when I tried to introduce her to the bottle. She clung to me when she changed classes in pre-school, and cried when we traded in our car. Time and time again, as she got older, she would tell us how she hated change. In the end, it was her family who had to endure the ultimate change.

While I was growing up, my mom would say, "I'm too old to change." I never quite understood what she meant, since she was changing every day. Deep thinking, I know, but isn't it true? Change seemed inevitable, as far as I could see. The realization occurred to me in young adulthood that the one thing we have control over, true control—until our mental capacity diminishes—is our thoughts. We can choose to change our thoughts or not.

The law of change states that everything is in the process of becoming something else. Change happens everywhere, constantly. Change happens in our environment and in our atmosphere. It happens inside and outside. So, too, in our lives, change is the one constant, along with our pattern of thought. Why is change so hard to embrace? Change is difficult to embrace in a world where we have little control. Not changing makes us feel comfortable and safe.

Through acknowledgment that change exists, we have the gift of awareness that change is inevitable in our lives. According to international bestselling author John Kehoe, "There are three main factors that are the causes of change in our life: choice, chance and crisis. All three carry power and have their own particular dynamic."

Inherently, choosing change makes us more comfortable with the Law of Change. Kehoe goes on to say, "Each of us will be faced with all three modes of change, but using choice allows us to navigate our life with greater dexterity, and it should be a whole lot more fun. Working with the dynamics of choice means embracing change as a constant reality in our life, being vigilant in looking for changes that would help us, and then being proactive in initiating them."

Socrates so wisely said, "The secret of change is to focus all of your energy, not on fighting the old, but on building the new." Businesses that fail to develop new products lose market share to those companies that develop innovative products and services. Tried and true products often fall victim to the ever-changing tides of the marketplace. Even in business, if we don't want to change, the world will change around us. What makes it easy to understand and accept this simple economic fact, but not apply the same truth to our personal lives?

I recently told my girls I believe that to have a successful marriage couples need to keep working on their relationships. I think relationships often fail because one or both parties stop trying. Like the business that thinks its product will always be desired in the marketplace, failure to grow and change will find us bankrupt in our relationships as well. Through choosing to change and grow over time, we have the opportunity for our relationships to flourish and deepen, not only with our spouse, but also with our children, family members, friends and co-workers.

To accept change as a constant, we need to accept that our physical bodies are subject to change as well. Sometimes we try to deny this simple fact. But, when we can no longer zip up our pants because of the extra pounds that somehow made their way onto our body, denial is no longer an option. Wouldn't it be great if we had the same type of obvious signs when it comes to our thoughts, like Beep . . . Beep . . . Beep . Warning!! Warning!! If we don't change those self-sabotaging thoughts, we will be unable to weather the storm ahead.

The great thing is that we possess the ability to forecast potential changes in our life and implement a storm preparedness program, before the next big one hits. Being aware that we can face different changes and challenges in life, allows us to create a mental preparation plan. After years of experiencing how my hair stylist handled the untimely passing of her daughter, I asked myself how I would handle that scenario if it happened to me. How could I go on and not be angry? Whenever my mom told me she was too old to change, I would ask myself what I can do to never turn my back to change when I grow up, even when life gets really hard? When we ask powerful questions, we'll find powerful answers that will guide us through the natural changes of our lives. By doing this, we exercise the power of our mind and unleash an acute awareness of the thoughts we entertain on a daily basis.

As for chance, Kehoe writes the following: "Chance is the word we use when we don't know or understand why something has happened to us." From a Mind Power perspective, very few things happen by pure chance. Ninety-five percent of the things that happen to us have their causes in our (conscious and subconscious) thoughts and our actions. There is a cause-and-effect relationship, though we might not always recognize it. We are on far better footing, both metaphysically and practically, if we assume responsibility for what is happening in our lives and get on with it, rather than believing that life's circumstances have nothing to do with us. Chance is like luck. And, yes, both exist. But, an excellent quote by A.J. Foyt, winner of the Indianapolis 500, sums up my feelings about luck: "Luck is when preparation meets opportunity… Initiate positive change in your life regularly and chance and luck will favor you."

In 2004, we were expecting our third child. In preparing for her arrival, we did a small remodel project at our home. Since the project included replacing a large portion of flooring, Paul and I decided to move our furniture to a local storage unit in town. After securing the space and taking out insurance for our belongings while they were being stored, we went on our merry way. Less than 24 hours later, the manager called and explained that there had been a fire in the unit next to us, and that many of our items had suffered fire damage. Even though we had the best intentions to keep our belongings safe, it was by chance that the unit next to ours happened to catch on fire.

Positive circumstances happen by chance as well. In 1992, I went on a cruise to the Caribbean with my mom, sister and a family friend. I was a young adult and had broken up with my long-term boyfriend just three months prior. Although I had no expectations of finding love on that trip, I happened to meet Paul, my future husband and love of my life. Of course, it was a series of thoughts and actions that made the meeting meaningful. There is personal responsibility in the form of our reaction and action to every chance happening in our lives.

The third type of change is thrust upon us out of crisis. Unfortunately, we all will experience some type of crisis in his or her life. Whether it's friendship drama when we're younger, relationship breakups, dissolution of marriage, business failings, job loss, health issues, natural disaster, or the untimely loss of a loved one, the effect is life altering.

There's nothing agreeable about something Earth shattering happening in your life. As I shared with you earlier, I knew the moment I stood at the train tracks and realized my beautiful Jenna was gone that I had major decisions to make regarding how we would move forward. As the months marched on after Jenna's passing and I began to accept our reality, I also began to understand that I had become more than I had ever been in my life. The crisis had broken me open. I became acutely in tune with my inner being. I was stripped from my ego. Jenna's passing un-Earthed what my soul's purpose is. It had been there all along. There's evidence of my purpose running throughout the theme of my life, yet I was blind to it. I had always been searching for 'it.' A crisis forces us to live in a space of truth. The circumstances are often irreversible. Yet, what most of us do not realize is that we hold the cards as to how we allow ourselves to change around those circumstances.

I began to ask myself powerful questions about how I could share my love for Jenna with the world and how I could pay forward all the love and support that had been given to our family. As a result of asking thoughtful questions, we co-founded the #hersmile nonprofit, whose mission is to bring hope, strength and inspiration to families who have experienced a tragedy like ours.

Prior to Jenna's passing, I did a lot of volunteer work. It was my way of contributing. However, my volunteer hours were mostly self-serving, since I volunteered at the school my children attended. After Jenna's passing, I wanted my contribution to have a broader reach. I wanted to impact the world in a more powerful way. I wanted to make sure Jenna's spirit and life were shared with the world. As her mother, I was left with the power, if I chose it, to create significant change from the crisis our family was to endure.

For most of us, change is not enjoyable. Yet it is through change that we have the greatest opportunity to grow. It forces us to change direction, self-assess, and consciously choose our path going forward. Oftentimes, inevitable change is a difficult process. It shakes our psyche and forces us to look at the life we have been living and the person we have become. It gives us the opportunity to become conscious. Ultimately, when we're able to choose a path of love and light despite our circumstances, we're able to realize what a gift we've been given.

I've asked myself many times if I would have chosen the path of light and love had Jenna not passed away. If God came to me and said I could have my daughter back right now, would I still chose to be the person I am today?

Would I still live my life wanting to share love and make my little part of the world a better place? Selfishly, I know I would want her back. I am certain, however, that Jenna has bestowed upon me the most amazing gift a daughter could give to her mother. She has opened our hearts and we are better people because of her. Kehoe concludes: "Comfort is the enemy of change, and when we are too comfortable in our present situation, we often resist the impulse to make change. A crisis dramatically forces that change upon us. It's always painful and never pleasant, but if accepted, it is ultimately healing and almost always beneficial."

Life has a way of breaking us open and transforming us. It's important to acknowledge change and the role it plays in our lives. Whether change occurs through choice, chance or crisis, do as Ghandi said: "Be the change you want to see in life." Create the life you want around the cards you are dealt.

When the Tides Have Calmed

It is only natural for people to go back to their regular lives after a tragic event has occurred. When visits from family and friends begin to wane, it's understandable to feel wracked with sadness and grief, as if the loss has just occurred all over again. When the external love that had previously held you up is distanced, you are now left to look inward in hope of soothing yourself. The stages of grief are universal, but they do not necessarily happen in a particular order. They are generally agreed to include denial and isolation, anger, bargaining, depression, and acceptance.

Due to the questions I had asked myself early on, I was able to recognize a path groomed with love and direction. At times, I felt deep sadness and pain, but I did not suffer from the reality of each stage. Instead, I entered each stage with acceptance and awareness. Echart Tolle beautifully recognized this process of acceptance in his book, *The Power of Now*, with these words: "If you cannot accept what is outside, then accept what is inside." He went on to say that if you cannot change what is happening outside yourself, then work to accept what is going on inside you. Feel every emotion and do not resist that which lies within you. Surrender to whatever emotion causes you pain. Become aware of it, but do not judge the emotion or yourself. Simply pay attention to it. Tolle goes on to say, "Then see how the miracle of surrender transmutes deep suffering in to deep peace. This is your crucifixion. Let it become your resurrection and ascension."

What a striking way to say what my golf coach had said all along, "Through awareness comes dissipation."

When we resist feelings of loss, ordering them to go away or demanding to know why they happened, they persist like a child tugging at his mother's leg to get her attention. When we become aware of the rhythm that guides our every move, we can sing through our emotions, as we find our way to a melody that resonates deep within our soul.

Chapter 5

Power of Beliefs

In some cultures, death elicits great pain and a sense of loss, while others celebrate the inherent rhythm of life and believe a soul reincarnates again and again on Earth until it becomes perfect and reunites with its Source. These two belief systems evoke substantially different internal emotions and experiences.

Our core beliefs largely determine the meaning we attach to the events in our life and how they shape our reality. Beliefs impact whether we have a lifetime of making joyous contributions or one of misery and devastation. Many leading authors in the field of self-development have discussed the impact that disempowering beliefs have on our lives. Motivational speaker and self-help author Tony Robbins said, "Our beliefs are like unquestioned commands."

Most people's beliefs are so embedded that they often neglect to notice their influence in their lives. Often, beliefs are inherited from their upbringing and/or life's situation. Rarely do individuals make a conscious choice about their belief system. When a tragedy strikes, the person is left to fall back on a belief system whereby, as in the case of the *Three Little Pigs*, you "huff and (you) puff and the whole house blows down."

Our internal beliefs surface at every turn but are recognized most when our lives are put to the test, and we are taken out of our comfort zone. If we haven't personally designed our beliefs prior to a painful event, it's highly likely that our flaws will rear their ugly heads in the form of depression, victimization, and lack of control.

Belief System

As we continue to practice awareness, we begin to observe, like a referee officiating a game, the thoughts and conversations that take place in our mind. Our beliefs may conjure up feelings of pain, when we are in a particular circumstance. Another person put in the same situation may feel pleasure or sustained inner peace. Is it all that simple? What we believe determines what we'll experience in life? Yep!

Our grief journey has led us to meeting other families who have lost children. I've interviewed several of them.

Those who believe they were entitled to have their children outlive them suffer more from their loss than those who believe they were given a treasure not marred by stipulation of time and place.

One dad believed that life never went his way. He found it impossible to think of anything besides the fact that his son's passing was just one more piece of evidence proving how horrible his life was. Another father, who believed all relationships in life were gifts, focused on the beautiful moments he and his son had shared with one another while together. Both dads had lost a son, but they reacted differently. Why? They had different belief systems!

The system shapes what thoughts we're willing to entertain, and those thoughts shape our experience. Metaphorically, it works like a recipe. Want to make an amazing berry pie over and over again? Or, maybe it's a chocolate lava cake that makes your heart sing. Whatever it is, learn what the ingredients are, the measurements, and what each step entails. If you do, the results will be the same every time! This is how a joyous, peaceful life works.

As you become aware of your belief system, notice the effect it has on the energy flowing through your body. What's amazing is that our beliefs create distinctive energy. Does that energy flow freely or lie stagnant in the murky waters of your thoughts? Do not judge either observation. Stand back and remain the silent observer. Slowly take deep breaths, in and out. The keys are: observe, remove the chatter, and do not judge. You must understand what comprises your foundation, before you can build the structure that will carry you forward to a life of peace and joy. What do you believe about the circumstances of your life? Just to be clear, your belief system is the foundation of who you are. It's through the understanding of self-discovery that you will begin to design the life you want and the contribution you want to make, despite your circumstances.

Controlled by Your Own B.S.

After Jenna's passing, I heard many people talk about how her life was unfairly cut short and that no parents should ever have to bury their child. I began to think about this belief. I understood from people's comments that, should I choose to live in despair, it would be justified because, after all, my child had died. The expectation in our culture that a parent would be forever broken over her loss was implicit.

A large part of the authentic human experience is masked by the human ego. We search for meaning in everything we do from that clouded vantage point, and then falsely define ourselves and the world around us. The subjective meanings we apply to life ultimately become our B.S.—Belief System.

Our beliefs determine the questions we'll even consider asking ourselves. If I believed that I had been cheated from living a long life with my child and deserved to experience every human milestone with her, would I or could I even consider moving on in a meaningful way? Would my B.S. guide me to ask limiting, debilitating questions? Or, would it allow me to ask empowering questions? The answer lies in the foundation of the B.S.

Our belief system is formed when we are young and builds over time. That is why so much of what we believe is so deeply rooted in our unconscious mind. The mind has an amazing ability to sort information and find patterns, which means we seek out evidence in the world to keep proving ourselves right. However, everything is sifted through a subjective brain, prejudiced from the start.

Our ongoing understanding of the world is based on our biased observations. The human brain has the phenomenal ability to take in large amounts of data, but processing that data happens at a slower rate, leaving large amounts on the cutting room floor. How do we determine what information we concentrate on and what we leave behind? The answer is simple. Our brain looks for patterns that reinforce and sort information, so the events are consistent with our beliefs. This helps us make sense of life. The brain sifts through all the information, like pieces to our own individual puzzle, weighing and placing value in accordance and validating our present beliefs. Information that doesn't fit is not considered and deleted.

Our belief system is very powerful. Beliefs can be debilitating or supportive, inspired by love, or mired in fear. For example, if I believed that I didn't deserve happiness, my brain would have immediately concluded that my daughter died because I did not deserve to be happy, so the loss was befitting. The conclusions we come to are ALWAYS based on our originating belief system. Our beliefs create our reality. It's fair, then, to say that life gives us nothing more than what we believe. This concept may read like a riddle; however, the beauty of riddles is they expand our mind and the way we look at the world.

Creating an Empowering Belief System

Since our brain has the capacity to process information only through the channels we tune in to, it must be true that beliefs are adjustable as well. If beliefs were fixed, all of humanity would have the same belief system. Right? Think about it. Why doesn't everyone believe what you believe? Why are there so many religions, political parties, and sports rivalries? Can you think of a person in your life who always sees the good in things, or perhaps it's easier for you to think of a person who, regardless of the circumstances, picks out the negative? No doubt we can all answer yes to both. It's the adage of the glass being half empty or half full. Since that's the case, I would argue that you have greater control over your belief system and the outcome of your life than you may realize.

A Meeting with Joanna

When we experience great loss, it's understandable to feel like a victim. Life has screwed us over, and there's nothing we can do about it. My belief system told me to take responsibility for my reaction to Jenna's passing and not render myself helpless. Believe me, I miss Jenna with every ounce of my being. There isn't a moment of the day when I don't miss her. Yet, I do not believe in living in darkness for the rest of my years. I believe all three of my daughters are gifts. I have so much love for my girls and my family. I believed I needed to show the world just how much love I have by openly expressing it. My self-talk was, and continues to be, empowering. I continue to ask myself what I can do to express the love for my children and my family out into the world.

Life always has a way of testing our core beliefs. I believe meeting Joanna was no coincidence. My grief counselor had invited me to hear her speak at a local chapter of a national grief organization. I was looking forward to it, because she was going to speak about grief and the signs that our loved ones give us after their passing. Her talk was uplifting and interactive. Many people, including myself, shared their stories and the signs they had received from their departed loved ones. As the evening was coming to a close, we prepared to leave. Just then, a lady from the audience came up to me and offered her condolences. She was very kind. She introduced herself as Joanna. I will never forget her. She was petite and had beautiful blue eyes. Her hair was short and she was bundled in a wool sweater. She shared with me that she had lost her son in a tragic mountain bike accident in Europe five years prior. Her energy was heavy. When she spoke, her eyes filled with tears. I could feel the depths of her pain and my heart broke for her. At the end of our conversation, she said, "You should come to one of our meetings. We all understand each other's suffering."

After thanking her, I gently replied, "What I've learned from Jenna's passing is that we all have some form of suffering in our lives. No one is immune to it. I believe it's really important for me to not stay in that space of suffering."

She hesitated. She did not acknowledge what I said. Her body language spoke for her. Her eyes bloodshot from crying. She had not identified with the words I'd just spoken. She shook my hand and said, "It was nice meeting you. I know the worst is yet to come for you."

I believe Joanna was trying to tell me that for her the road of grief had been long and that time hadn't taken away her suffering. While I could have internalized this, given my vulnerable state, I told myself to let it go. I did not, nor would I, choose to accept that as my reality. We had very distinct belief systems. We both had lost a child. However, we have chosen to move on in dramatically different ways. I learned a great lesson that night. I continued to believe in hope for what the best could be and what I could create, regardless of my circumstances.

Again, we ascribe meaning to our lives based on what we believe and what we consider possible. *Do not make the mistake of adopting someone else's belief as your own.* Become conscious of your beliefs, and design the experience you want to create out of your own circumstances.

Leverage Beliefs

Nothing can stop you, except your beliefs. Expectations also play a significant role. The first great challenge to understanding your beliefs is to accept that many of them are housed in the subconscious. We will explore more about opening your subconscious to your awareness, but for now understand that many of your core beliefs were taught to you, you were exposed to them via the media, or you developed them early on from your interpretation of your experiences.

Different sets of beliefs aren't a matter of coincidence or good fortune. They are a direct result of "united energy." United energy is the alignment of beliefs and expectations. My beliefs are that our lives mean something special; we are part of a greater whole, and we experience this physical life to grow closer to the light and love of our Creator. These beliefs allow me to have the expectation of a meaningful, loving life, despite

Jenna's passing. These beliefs, which are based in love, tap into a high vibrational universal energy that, by its own design, has led me on a path of love and inspired action.

Unfortunately, Joanna's belief system surrounding the loss of her son had thrust her onto a low vibrational plane tarnished by suffering and depression. In his book, *Think and Grow Rich,* Napoleon Hill, author and teacher on the principles of success, wrote, "Whatever the mind of man can conceive and believe, it can achieve." This is what it means to leverage your beliefs. Although I'll never know exactly what Joanna's belief system is, I did learn that her thoughts about suffering caused her to experience life in this manner.

It Takes a Large Shovel

Yes, it takes a large shovel to unearth the plethora of subconscious beliefs, but it's worth the effort. Being able to identify your empowering and disempowering beliefs is essential, if you wish to bring about lasting change. In order to take responsibility for the outcome of all aspects of your life, you'll have to make some change in your beliefs. Let me make clear that what you experience is, and should be, separate from your life's circumstances. Very few people make the distinction that what is happening externally can be different from what is happening internally.

When facing the untimely loss of a loved one, or any trauma for that matter, our unconscious belief system goes into autopilot. Without awareness at high alert, our B.S. can take us where we do not want to go. Many who read this book understand all too well the depths of suffering that can be experienced after a loss. Taking action to change our disempowering beliefs changes our perception of reality, and it will change our overall experience. Letting go of disempowering beliefs is challenging—sometimes scary—but worth it.

Know Thyself

Throughout history, great thinkers have proclaimed the wisdom associated with knowing thyself. The broader meaning suggests the need to take an active role in your own personal self-discovery. Self-reflection and introspection are means to understanding one's human nature.

If you truly want to live a fulfilling and happy life, despite your circumstances, you must live in harmony with your true values. The challenge is that we didn't consciously choose most aspects of our value system. Values make up the ego essence of who we are. Your values are what you've prioritized in your life as being important. To understand what makes you really 'You,' ask yourself what you value most in life. Write down and prioritize your top 10 values.

If I asked you what was most important, you might answer family, money and health as your top three values. If I asked you to expound on why you value family, you might answer: the feelings of love and connection it generates and brings to your life. Is it possible to get love and connection outside your family? Absolutely!

Understanding the underlying emotions and subsequent feelings that your values allow you to experience is important, as you navigate the ups and downs of life and learn to create a meaningful and loving existence, despite your circumstances. This can only happen through awareness. As you become aware, you will experience what it feels like for a blind person, when given the gift of sight. Through deeper understanding and self-awareness, you will be able to experience soul-soothing emotions, like love and connection beyond the family unit, because you will have had your eyes opened to the emotional responses you seek in your life. You'll be able to experience them via your own internal direction and creation. This is another piece of life's great puzzle. Creating the life you want, despite your circumstances, is achievable.

The Root of Suffering

When we experience something devastating, our world radically alters. Not only are our circumstances forever changed, so is the image we have of ourselves. Ego orients how we view ourselves in the world. Metaphorically, ego is the vehicle (our physical self). Our belief system makes up the unique characteristics of our vehicle (each of which comes with a special package of options). The combination of the two, the physical self and the bells and whistles on the inside, make up who we are.

For example, I (ego) am (a)_____ and I believe (belief system) _____.

Write down five to 10 sentences using the fill-in sentence above. Exercises like this help you explore how you define yourself.

All humans create an image of what they are in the world. One of the most difficult things about change is that it challenges how we define ourselves. When we are a parent and our child dies, we may feel like that role has been stripped away from us. "Who am I, if I am not a mother or a father?" Or, if our partner dies, we may find ourselves in a pile of rubble of a different sort.

Many of our beliefs about how we define ourselves also shape the potential experiences we afford ourselves. When I stopped playing competitive golf, one of the hardest things for me was the shift in my identity. Who was 'I,' if I was no longer a golfer? As time went on, I learned that I had shaped my life around what I did, versus who I was. I soon realized that the ego identifies with 'what' you do. For example: I am a mother. I am a father. I am a business owner.

Our roles and relationships in life are important, yet we are more. We are part of the bigger whole, the universal energy. As we begin to peel away the layers of our ego and connect with universal energy, we begin to understand how everything is possible. The only truths are love, compassion and kindness. It is through this truth that healing is possible. We are pure love. Although our human experience challenges us time and again, we can resonate with the light within and live in a place of joy and gratitude.

Humans are very good at allowing their egos to determine a perception of how they fit in with the larger picture. It is our way of making sense of the world. The paradox is that our energy is the same potential energy that flows through all living beings. Creating a fulfilling life despite our circumstances requires us to disconnect at will from our ego, the part that falsely defines who we are, based on what we do and what we have, compared to the world around us.

I will teach you how to how connect with universal energy and disconnect from your ego. This lesson is vital, because it's your ego wherein suffering lies.

Inside of You is a World of Thoughts

Ego is a metaphysical, Latin word that means "the self; that which feels, acts, or thinks," or "I." The great philosophers and psychologists throughout time have studied its origins and role in the human experience. Ego causes some of the greatest problems. So, why is ego so important to your grieving heart? Again, when ego is in command of your life, it defines who you are and the circumstances that surround you. When struck with the ever so impactful loss of a loved one, the reverberation of your loss may have crippling affects over your perception of 'self.' It's the ego that ignites feelings of anger, failure, self-pity, fear, jealousy and victimization. When ego is in command, you separate from the continuum of life and death. Ultimately, you label your loved one's death as a personal assault against you.

Very little conversation addresses life's inherent struggles and roadblocks. What if you shared your life's challenges with others? Would you begin to understand that adversity happens to everyone? Would your ego surrender? Would everything cease to feel so personal? Would you come to understand that it's through hardship that your sense of who you are has the greatest opportunity for personal growth? Have you ever been around a person who starts opening up about their personal struggles, and the next thing you find yourself doing is opening up about your own hardships? If the answer is yes, then you've experienced the act of letting go of your ego.

Since Jenna passed, many people have expressed to me how our loss, the death of a child, was more significant than any other loss or hardship someone could experience. Time and time again, I have responded that I've come to understand that we all have challenges, problems and heartache. Nobody is exempt. When you separate yourself from your ego, you can begin to understand that the continuum of life and death is not personal. It's not an assault against you. It's natural law at work.

Under the Bodhi Tree

My introduction to Buddhism was valuable. Don't get me wrong. I'm not an expert by any means, but meditation is something I continue to work on, so I can become more aware of my thinking. Our ego often rears its head with thoughts of self-pity and self-judgment. As we move through grief or hardships, there is less and less room for negative, egocentric beliefs. Buddhists ascribe to the notion that we cling to things we believe will make us happy or keep us safe. Eventually, though, we will be disappointed, because everything is impermanent, everything changes. Plans we look forward to come and go, people travel in and out of our lives, and every day the sun manages to rise and set. Change is impersonal, even when it doesn't feel that way.

Months prior to Jenna's Sweet 16 birthday, we began planning for a Twilight Gala that was to be held in honor of this milestone, wrapped in the silver lining of raising charitable funds for the nonprofit we had started in

Jenna's memory. We spent months of preparation, and I looked forward to honoring Jenna and showing my love for her. The two weeks that followed the fun, hugely successful event, brimming with love, left me feeling completely empty. What shifted in me to cause me to feel this void?

As we open our soul to the love and light of our Creator and free our ego from filling every moment with superficial pursuits, material possessions, and life's dramas, our light grows larger. We get to the core of who we truly are. At that moment, we come face to face with our soul's calling. As we grieve the loss of our loved ones, it is difficult to grasp a greater plan. However, great spiritual teachers speak of such a notion. The true destination of every soul is to give of itself to others. The emptiness created by change creates an expansiveness within us that allows us to see life in a whole new light. It opens possibilities we would never have considered prior to the change.

As Buddha learned thousands of years ago, the only way to get through the pain is to *be* with it, for even pain is impermanent. So, for two weeks after our event, I just sat with the emptiness. I didn't push it away or try to mask it by running away from it. I sat with it, I felt it, and it walked away on its own. I didn't try to overanalyze or fix it. I told my ego to step to the side and self-pity not to knock on my door. I meditated, calmed my mind, and continued to remind myself that within emptiness there is fullness. We truly can't know one without the other. Once we understand that we exist within this container of duality, we'll begin to understand that we have power greater than we ever realized. Every experience in life is intended to lead us to grow in love, compassion and kindness. Our circumstances aren't intended to break us. Rather, they are intended to break us open, so we choose to 'be' in the light and love of our Creator despite our circumstances. We choose to 'be' more than our superficial pursuits and egocentric selves. There is nothing in this world that can fill the emptiness besides this truth:

"As we experience ego death at a personal and societal level, many people panic, thinking this is the end of the world. Yet it is not – it's just the snake shedding its skin. What's really happening is that the way you identify yourself is changing from a limited sense of self to a very expanded one." — Penney Peirce

Who I Am is No Longer Working for Me

As you begin to dis-identify with your ego, like a snake shedding its skin, do not be surprised if you begin to contemplate the question that has intrigued humans for thousands and thousands of years: Who am I? The simple answer is: "I am part of the whole, the love and light of our Creator." You come to the physical realm to realize and transcend your understanding of self.

Dr. Michael Newton holds a doctorate in counseling psychology, a certificate in master hypnotherapy and is the author of *Journey of Souls: Case Studies of Life Between Lives*. He writes: "We are divine but imperfect beings who exist in two worlds, material and spiritual." He goes on to say that our main purpose for our physical existence is to master ourselves and to acquire knowledge. It's a process that takes time, patience and determination, because there are so many challenges inherent on the Earthly plane. It's a challenge for us to realize our true essence, because we're constantly faced with the challenges of living, inhabiting our physical bodies, the environment, and encountering emotions and egocentric thoughts. Still, we never lose our true self.

It's understandable that people feel a sense of hopelessness about the meaning of life and who they are, when they are forced to endure life's harsh realities. Our capacity for self-transcendence is often hindered by such circumstances, thus our inability to break through our wounds and egocentrism.

Yet, there is more than this earthly, linear plane. The idea that we exist in a multidimensional space that is evident all around us, such as the hundreds of documented near-death experiences. These accounts have further illustrated that there is more to this physical space than meets the eye. The spirit world exists and we come to Earth to grow our knowledge, evolve the vibration of our soul to a higher level, and to understand that our true essence is one with the light and love of our Creator. At this point you may be wondering why such a cruel school exists. That's a fair question.

Our entire life is spent shedding our outer layer of skin in pursuit of what matters most. We are given the ability to understand the true essence of our being through opportunities and experiences in a physical space, where we come to realize that the only truth is love. No superficial pursuits matter. The process of self-mastery takes patience and determination.

I often pray that I learn the lessons I'm supposed to learn in this lifetime. I ask myself whether I can grieve with love in my heart, without being bitter or broken. And I pose, "What can I do to express my love for Jenna and my family in the world?" It's not easy to shed the outer layers of who I perceive myself to be, but I have surrendered. Now, I ask for a higher power to guide me. What I have experienced has been a beautiful self-transcendence.

"I" Am Changing

After the storm of a personal tragedy and trauma rips through our life, we are left with very little certainty about who we are. We cannot initially clarify life's purpose. This season wreaks havoc, leaving its victims susceptible to illness, depression, and emptiness.

This transformational time also clears the canvas, allowing the dissolution of the things we don't need. We begin to see that the external world does not define us and that we are connected to the universal energy of unconditional love, which is the highest vibration with which we can align. We are more than our possessions, financial status and titles. We are more than our tragedies, traumas and hardships. During this time, life is preparing us for the rebirth of the new self. This can happen many times in life.

Once we've accepted the fact that nothing we can do will bring back our loved one or recreate the former external conditions, we start to experience freedom from our ego. Right off, we want to fill this space with activity and return to what has been comfortable, because the idea of being quiet with our grief and pain frightens us. When stripped of our identity, we fear even more loss. That is ego begging us not to let go. The amazing thing about being in the quietness is that we strip ourselves down to the true self. We are transformed into a masterpiece of grace, strength and love. Quietness allows us to be more than we ever were before. We are more than the voice inside, more than the tragedies and traumas we've experienced. It is vital not to fill the space of quietness, but just *be* in it.

I remember being stripped of my identity after Jenna passed away. I knew myself as the mother to three girls, not two. I owned my own business. I contributed to our financial bottom line. I took care of my girls and my husband. I kept the household running. I was a doer. I was a volunteer. I was a fun person. Yet, aside from my loving and taking care of my family, nothing else mattered to me. My ego had been shot to smithereens. I felt empty, as if "I" no longer existed.

I began to find solace in being in nature and hiking in Northern California's East Bay hills. Early one day, I was hiking a ridgeline with my dog, Pepper. We encountered a majestic grove of ancient oak trees. Their branches stretched over the horizon as the green moss that adorned them glistened in the dawning of the sun. Their beauty penetrated me. I reflected on the symbolism of strength and endurance that the tree signifies. At that moment, it came to me that all these wonderful masterpieces had to do each day was grow to their highest potential. Just then, I realized that these mesmerizing trees had endured the harshest of storms, and yet they continued to grow and their roots continued to strengthen. Like a tree growing toward the light of the sun, I gave myself permission to grow toward the love and light of our Creator. I prayed to Jenna, asking her to show me the way. I prayed for the wisdom and courage to walk through the doors that had opened before me.

Being stripped of ego can be very painful. However, it allows us to embark on a trip into an authentic world of self-discovery and moves us towards our highest personal vibrational level. Each one of us has a true nature and path to follow. Like the mighty oak tree, we all weather storms in our lives. With the intention of continuing to grow daily to our greatest potential, we gain grace, connection and love, as our branches continue to grow toward the realization of our destiny.

Why Am I here? (Clue) For a Reason

Problems and difficulties can bring out the stronger character traits in all of us. Everyone faces struggles in life. That is what growth is all about. The bottom line is that your energy has a positive contribution to make and a purpose to fulfill. By utilizing your own personal energy, which is Life itself, and living each moment to the fullest, you use your energy to fulfill your soul's purpose.

I remember getting the call from my college coach and having him offer me a golf scholarship. I remember being reacquainted with Paul, my now husband, after not seeing him for several years. Around these circumstances, it was as if there was some cosmic opening of doors and it felt obvious that I was to walk through them and take the opportunities being presented to me. I also remember the ease we had in growing our family. All these occasions were magical. Everything seemed to unfold so seamlessly. Those were such beautiful times in my life.

On the contrary, I remember trying so hard to be an amazing golfer. The emotional struggles I endured are hard to reflect on even now. I was also in a long-term relationship that felt one-sided and subservient. I put so much of everything I had into making both perfect, yet time and time again I ran into one obstacle after another, and this time instead of doors opening, I felt the impact of them closing.

Are you aware of the opportunities and struggles that have occurred in your life? Life leaves clues as to the direction you should take. If you don't follow the clues, emotional upheaval and imbalance prevails.

Everyone is born with potential and something positive to contribute to the Universe, as well as something to glean from it. We are free to deal with circumstances and people in our lives with whatever part of our character we choose, but peace of mind, success, contentment, fulfillment and spirituality occur only when our energy is balanced. Only then can we express the essence that makes up our true self.

Awareness of precisely where the balance lies is learned through experience. If, in a previous life, we chose to leave our potential undeveloped, thereby contributing nothing to the health of the Universe, then the next life brings with it a strong urge to rectify the imbalance. This pull is referred to as Karmic Lessons.

The universal vibration, or fate, provides us with certain sets of life circumstances. In doing so, we experience various facets of our Karmic Lessons, which are never meant to punish. They are meant to bring everything back into balance. This experience enables us to develop our personal awareness. Repeatedly facing a particular set of circumstances or struggles gives us the opportunity to eventually realize that the only one possible solution is a balanced method of coping. This is what brings harmony to all things.

For example, I learned about Karmic Lessons from a numerologist, years before Jenna passed away. She did my chart and shared that one of my Karmic Lessons causes me to experience feelings of loneliness, fear, sadness, and self-doubt. I am being required to find faith in myself and my own inner guidance to restore my alignment. The challenge is compounded by my skepticism and overly intellectual approach to life. So, I must learn to trust in myself, in others, and in the metaphysical world. The numerologist also shared with me that finding balance can be challenging, but when we do, our lessons bring faith, peace of mind, serenity, wisdom, awareness, knowledge and poise into our lives. The irony is, if she hadn't shared this information with me, I am confident that I would have expressed what I thought my life's lessons were in much the same way.

What life lessons do you still have to learn? What clues lead you to believe that those are your lessons?

What's even more eerie about what the numerologist shared with me was that my lesson could be the result of an attitude of excessive skepticism—a refusal to acknowledge the reality of the God-force or unseen world in one of my previous lives. Or, if my energy was inactive in a previous life, I may have lived adhering to orthodox religious ideology, having unrealistic faith in my religion, but not necessarily having faith in a higher power, nor any belief in myself. So, this life experience has brought situations where loss, sorrow, grief or isolation occurs. There is no one to turn to in times of need, until I realize that turning within to search my innermost being is the only way to cope. Crazy! Right? I'd say so. Although I've always had a sense that we are here for a reason, there's so much evidence validating that inner intuition.

Now, let's be clear. Everyone's lessons are completely different. We all have experienced great loss, but what I've learned from my experience may be the polar opposite of what you need to learn. The idea of Karma is quite complex. Simply put, our souls seek to evolve by encountering experiences in the physical realm. We incarnate over many lives and repeat the cycles, until our soul reaches a point of mastery over the lower energy vibrations, and we seek balance and wisdom in all of our experiences.

The universal law of cause and effect, Karma, states in several religions in some form that you reap what you sow. The idea is to learn your lessons in this lifetime by not over-using or under-using your energy around the lesson. Once balance is achieved, the lesson is complete and you're free to move on to new experiences.

Use the imbalance in your life as a springboard for growth in the present. Everything you need to move forward is balanced by love. How do you know if you've mastered the lesson? Easy! The same negative scenarios stop repeating in your life.

There is no "bad" Karma! However, personal experience of the out-of-harmony or out-of-balance state can be felt through pain and suffering. All pain is felt only when one is either over-using or under-using personal energy. What in the world does that mean? Take, for example, something that has challenged me repeatedly in my life—being sensitive to other people's apathy, their choices, and how they treat me. Over-expending part of my energy takes me to a mental place of insensitivity. Under-using part of my energy causes me to take things too personally. The balanced part of my energy allows me to be diplomatic, gentle and sincere. All suffering is overcome by expressing harmonious and balanced energy.

It is your own personal responsibility to work on finding that harmony. Let me repeat, it is *your* responsibility to find harmony in your life. Despite the pain of Jenna's passing, it was my job to cope with her passing in a way that didn't destroy my life or the lives of my family. It was my job to find balance within my emotions. And, the only way to achieve that balance is through unconditional love of yourself and the world around you. The ultimate destination for a soul on Earth is to live in a space of love and contribution, despite our human experience.

So, the answer to, "Why am I here?" is: I am here to learn lessons, to be a loving being, gain knowledge, and achieve harmony and balance. Period!

Chapter 7

The question is not whether you're going to
have problems, but how you're going to deal
with them when they come up.

-Tony Robbins

Intention: Broken Open

In his book *The Power of Intention: Learning to Co-create Your World Your Way*, Dr. Wayne W. Dyer wrote about being moved by two sentences he read in a book by Carlos Castaneda, while waiting to have a cardiac procedure. In *The Active Side of Infinity*, Castaneda wrote: "Intent is a force that exists in the universe. When sorcerers (those who live of the Source) beckon intent, it comes to them and sets up the path for attainment, which means that sorcerers always accomplish what they set out to do."

Those words had the same effect on me. They express everything I've come to understand. Our intention is the force we place on our life's energy, which is all around us and within us. It is the essence of our being, our consciousness, our soul. Life's energy flows through our physical, emotional, and spiritual bodies. The intentions will always become our reality.

If you want your grieving heart to mend, have the intention to mend it by moving forward with love, both by giving and receiving it. The power of intention is a field of energy that exists in all living things. It exists in YOU! Intention cannot be accessed through ego. We now understand that it can only be called upon from the source of our being, life's energy.

Again, it is our responsibility to find harmony in life. The only way to do that is to have the intention to move with the universal energy that we all belong to and away from ego dominance. When slower energies move through us, we may experience a sense of hopelessness. When we harmonize our thoughts and energy with the higher, faster universal energy field, we connect with spirit. The way to make this connection is through love, compassion and kindness for self and others.

Our Door Is Open

As I shared with you, Jenna's passing was an utter shock. In the morning, she was with us. By late afternoon she was gone. We had no time to mentally prepare. Yet, I knew instinctively that I could not let her death destroy us. I feel blessed to have had that intention from the outset. Embracing the power of my intention allowed the light and love of our highest energy source to shed its magnificent light on our path. It allowed us to receive the assistance we needed and desired. The manifestation of this came in the form of personal connection through the love we received from our family, friends and community.

On a spiritual level, I had a deep inner knowing that I was to keep our door open to those who came to our home to share their unconditional love with our family. Remember, the universe gives you clues. I could have used my free will to push people away, but that would have been counterintuitive to my greater intention. The universe pushed the love of people's energy in our direction. As Castaneda said, "The sorcerers always accomplish what they set out to do." It also meant putting aside our pride and accepting months upon months of meals that were given to us. It was through people's unconditional love that we could endure a pain so strong its wreckage seeped into our souls. It was through their unconditional love that my own soul was realized. I recognized that our emotional connections allow our soul to remember the purpose of its incarnation. The soul has a destiny. Our ability to give and receive unconditional love is the framework of our true essence. Our ability to let love in and let love out in harmony and balance represents the cycle of our universal energy and the way to our heart.

Family, friends and community members flowed into our home like the waters pouring through the banks of the Truckee River. Renee Travis, a formidable woman in her own right and my daughters' award-winning teacher, took the step to start the Jenna Betti Memorial Fund. Word about the fund traveled quickly and financial generosity followed. Little did she know that her act of unconditional love and kindness would shape how our family would draw meaning from our beautiful daughter's death. Oftentimes, people want to help, but they are at a loss when it comes to knowing what to do. Their ego, which is clad in judgment and fear, may stop

111

them from taking action, but I promise you that, as long as your actions are based in love, there is no right or wrong way to reach out. Never forget that your actions can change the course of someone's life. In this case, they changed ours.

The Creation of Intention

Now I know that one of my greatest intentions arose from my belief that it would be impossible to pay back all that had been given to our family. From the cards, the flowers, and the meals, to monetary donations and pink ribbons wrapped around trees throughout our community, there was no way I could properly thank everyone for what they had done for our family. I had to figure out a way to express my gratitude to the world.

We all have free will. I could have closed my eyes to all the love that had been wrapped around us and instead concentrated on our loss. Or, I could harness the love and gratitude within myself and share it with the world. My creative impulse was to pay forward all that had been given to us. As days turned into weeks, my treasured friends would continue to sit with me around my kitchen table. They allowed me to share how moved I was by the generosity of our family, friends and community. The more we talked, the more my state of unity grew with our

Creator. We are always making choices. I chose to witness the dissolution of my ego. I could sense that my choices regarding how to move forward had been propelled to a higher vibration and were inspired by pure love.

Love Takes Flight

When our intention is in harmony with love, kindness and compassion, we move toward the full expression of life and self. As I contemplated what I wanted, which was to pay forward all the love that had been given to us, I focused less on what I didn't have, Jenna in physical form. Manifestation of my intention took flight one evening as I sat at my kitchen table with two very close friends. As the creative energy of the universe filled the room, the idea of starting a nonprofit to help families thrust into a tragic loss like ours came to life. The moment was magical. Intention is like having a magic key that unleashes the creative power of the universe within you. I had focused so hard on how I could share my love and gratitude with my family, friends and community that the universe surrounded me with those who could help bring that to fruition. I experienced the formless field of energy, which powers intention. It manifests with ease, when you transcend your ego and come from a place of love, kindness and gratitude.

I had heard so much about Jenna's smile after she passed. Her smile could light up a room. She made you feel good just by being in her presence. After learning what friends and family had to say about her, I started hashtagging 'hersmile' on social media and soon friends and family followed suit. It seemed only fitting that we would name our nonprofit #hersmile. I feel honored to be a part of an organization that has stepped into such a painful arena. It's our mission to bring hope, strength and inspiration to those who have experienced the tragic loss of a child, or to a dependent child who has experienced the loss of a parent. Each time I receive an email request for assistance, my heart aches, for I understand what the grief journey entails. Yet, my resolve grows stronger every day. My intention is to show those with a grieving heart that grief, although extremely personal, does not have to ruin you. You do not have to live the rest of your days in darkness and despair, because of the ultimate power intention has in your life. Love is a powerful gift, and every life makes a difference in the universe.

To learn more about #hersmile, please visit www.hersmile.org.

Divine Time

Upon reflection, I realized that I had been preparing most of my life for this desire to pay forward all the love that had been given to us. I spent more than a decade volunteering and owning and operating several small businesses. Now, it seems not so coincidental that the culmination of all those years of experience would be to start a nonprofit that is rooted not just in our executive board's and my experiences. Most important, it is also rooted in volunteerism, contribution, love, compassion, and giving back. The same holds true for you. The culmination exists in order for your soul to grow and learn. Everything happens in a season and for a reason. Everything you need to know lies within your soul, yet the challenge is this: we must accept that everything happens according to Divine time, even the passing of our loved ones.

Years ago, I read a passage from Tony Robbins' book, *Awaken the Giant Within*. Robbins' son experienced the tragic loss of a classmate in elementary school. With deep compassion for his son's heartache, Robbins shared a story about how within every caterpillar lies a butterfly. We all have moments when we are caterpillars and don't know how to think any differently, because that is all we know. Then, one day the caterpillar thinks it has died, because it no longer resembles who it used to be in physical form. All the other caterpillars think it has died too. In reality, the caterpillar is merely transforming. One day the caterpillar breaks through its cocoon, dries off its wings and flies! It is now a beautiful butterfly. So often in life we don't understand the true beauty and potential that lies within each one of us. Robbins ended the story saying, "You see, it's not for us to decide when somebody becomes a butterfly. We think it's wrong, but I think God has a better idea when the right time is."

I understand that trusting in the perfection of every moment in your life is very difficult. It's difficult to trust in a world of hardships and heartaches, but the beauty of divine intention exists within you. Trust that every experience and lesson you learn in this lifetime happens to help your soul grow and realize its true Self. You may see yourself only as a caterpillar, but your soul takes flight during transformation and realization of your true essence. Remember, the beauty and freedom of a butterfly lies within you.

Brick by Brick

Setbacks and growth occur in small or big steps throughout your life. For example, the caterpillar emerges as a beautiful butterfly only after going through a very specific transformation. The same holds true for us. Every thought takes us either toward or away from healing or our expressed intention. I declared early on that I would live in accordance with my love for Jenna and project my love and gratitude out into the world. As floods of thoughts swept through my mind, my intention always brought me back to: "Focus on the love." However, before we can guide our thoughts, we must first be aware of the thoughts we are entertaining and come to understand that we are manifesting them. If we want to live a life in pure alignment with our intentions, the thoughts we contemplate must align with them.

Again, what we believe will ultimately be what we experience. The process of grieving can place a heavy fog over our intentions and our intended direction. The pain of losing a loved one can be debilitating and dark if you allow it. The pain of your traumas can leave you feeling helpless and worthless. The famous martial artist Bruce Lee said, "Defeat is a state of mind; no one is ever defeated until defeat has been accepted as a reality." I have been hesitant to join grief groups, primarily because of the possible disconnect with my intention. Since my intention is to live in my love and gratitude for Jenna and my family, conversations about the pain associated with her passing are not conducive to the path I've chosen.

It isn't that I do not have pain and heartache. I do. It is just that I understand from a lifetime of training my thoughts, that when we concentrate on what is missing in our life, our mind will continue to filter out all the good and show us evidence to prove we are right.

In his book, *The Happiness Advantage*, Shawn Achor wrote: "As a society, we know very well how to be unwell and miserable and so little about how to thrive. The point is . . . what we spend our time and mental energy focusing on can indeed become our reality."

The darkness, despair and sadness that accompany grief are directly related to feelings of purpose and meaning that also pass with our loved ones. If our intention is to live a life of joy and purpose again, we must have the corresponding thoughts to do so.

Ask yourself this question, "Would I trade the experience with my child or my loved one, if I knew they were going to die before me?" If you answer 'no,' then consider having as your intention to celebrate the gift your loved one gave you, and understand that he or she will always be in your life. Ask yourself, "How can I express my love and gratitude for my loved one out into the world?" The one you lost has made your life richer and more beautiful. The love you have for them will never die, nor will love's richness and beauty ever die.

Psychologist Barbara Fredrickson has coined the "Broaden and Build Theory." Her research found that positive emotions broaden the amount of possibilities we process, making us more thoughtful, creative and open to new ideas. Furthermore, positive emotions flood our brain with chemicals that make us feel good. From both a spiritual and mental perspective, we must harness our thoughts and link them with our intentions. Once our thoughts are in alignment with the love of our universal energy, the soul's purpose and intention will begin to unfold.

The final chapters of this book offer tools to help you connect with the pure love that resides within you and connect with your spirit guides who will help you identify your soul's purpose.

Chapter 8

"The two most important days in your
life are the day you are born and the
day you find out why."
-Mark Twain

Connecting with Your Soul

Having a strong sense of your destiny may be a foreign
concept to you. Let's face it, we are not brought up
learning how to explore why we are here or to determine
our larger purpose. When we were young, we did not
work on heightening our conscious awareness and coping
skills. Instead, we filled our minds with information. I'm
not at all discounting the importance of knowledge. It is
one of my highest values in life. Rather, I am pointing out
the difference between mere information gathering and a
process of connecting the dots, learning how to apply
what we learn in life, and discovering how to live from a

place within our souls. This place is fueled by love and compassion.

When our intention is to live in vibrational harmony with our destiny, we experience a joy that transcends our human experience, our grief and our hardships. Everyone experiences chaos and discord at one point or another. When we learn how to connect to our purpose and destiny, we'll rid ourselves of the shackles of ego and gravitate to an energy that radiates the joyful appreciation that loves to help us fulfill the spiritual contract we made with ourselves before we incarnated.

Jean-Yves Leloup, author of *Compassion and Meditation: The Spiritual Dynamic Between Buddhism and Christianity*, wrote: "Sometimes we must undergo hardships, breakups, and narcissistic wounds, which shatter the flattering image we had of ourselves, in order to discover two truths: that we are not who we thought we were; and that the loss of a cherished pleasure is not necessarily the loss of true happiness and well-being."

The soul's purpose is deeply spiritual in nature. That purpose is to deepen awareness, which helps us realize the greater wholeness within. It is through experiencing every human emotion that the potential to raise our vibrational energy exists and offers the opportunity to truly know ourselves. Metaphorically, if life is the classroom, it is our task to pass the test by harnessing our internal love, compassion and peace. Should we fail to rid ourselves of fear, judgment and disharmony, we may need to repeat the lesson until we achieve harmony.

Our soul's challenges may not only unfold in what we do each day, but may also include what we focus on internally, including our emotional states. Have you ever wondered why some people who seem to have it all are miserable? This is attributable to their internal emotional state wreaking havoc on them. Without exception, life presents our soul with the same lessons again and again, until your awareness heightens and we lift the illusion of our suffering and choose a life of love and harmony with all things.

Our soul's purpose is also connected to others. The opportunity to learn is invariably through our relationships and our experiences with the physical world and each other. Souls come together to further each other's learning and to reach the next level of vibrational energy that helps them become aware that they are one with the love and light of our highest energy source, our Creator, and to have the highest awareness of self. It is through our experiences that we become aware that we are more than our emotions. We are greater than our physical circumstances. At the core of our being we are not happy or sad, rich or poor, loving or hateful, empty or full, ugly or beautiful, dark or light. We are that which has no opposite—unconditional love. Every other state or emotion is impermanent.

To know thyself is to strip away the shackles of your emotions. I learned this valuable lesson from Jenna and her passing. Despite desperately missing her and the pain I have felt every day since her death, I realized that my existence was greater than my emotions. It was through my unconditional love for Jenna, my family and the world around me that I began to understand this valuable lesson of self. Did my emotions define the essence of my being? Was I a dark and devastated person, if I felt that way? My answer was, "Only if you allow your 'self' to 'be' those emotions." So, if I allowed myself to be a particular emotion, who was I apart from that emotion? The question was profound.

As I continued to reflect on philosophical questions like these and on my feelings for Jenna and her passing, I asked myself if it made sense to live out the rest of my days bitter, broken and disenchanted, when that wasn't at all how I felt about my daughter. Why such dichotomy in my feelings? Was I more than the sum of my emotions? When I stripped away the heartache, what remained? The profound answer was unconditional love.

This realization has had a profound impact on my life, as it will on yours. Despite my daily emotions, I continually bring my focus back to how I can express my true essence and unconditional love out into the world. I'm not suggesting this is easy work. It's been one of the greatest challenges and one of the richest rewards I have ever experienced. I have been repeatedly tested since Jenna's passing by people and circumstances in my life. It is only through unconditional love for self and the people and world around me that I have unearthed my soul's destiny.

Doors continue to open since I made this realization. I have seen the culmination of my life's experience and contributions take shape into something much grander. It was then that I unlocked the destiny of my soul and was led to co-found our nonprofit and write this book. For you, it might mean contributing your talents, gifts and heart in another way. Or, perhaps in the same way. When you begin to understand that the destiny of your soul is to project unconditional love to other people, yourself, and the world around you, despite your hardships, emotions, and life's circumstances, your soul will be blessed with its greatest gift, the gift of knowing thyself. There's a season and reason for everything that happens in our lives, all helping us to realize our essence of unconditional love.

Still Searching

Singer/songwriter Adele's gift has radiated since early childhood. Door after door opened up for her, so she could realize her soul's destiny. There are examples of prodigies in every profession. From the outside, these individuals look as if they have everything from fame and fortune to happiness. But, they are only able to live out their destiny in peace and harmony, if their gifts are rooted in unconditional love for themselves, their aptitudes, and the world around them. We are reminded throughout history—from Ludwig Van Beethoven to Michael Jackson—that talent alone is not a remedy for life's hardships or life's joys. Every soul that walks this earth has something to give, some contribution to make, and challenges to overcome.

Unlike the prodigal talents that have walked this Earth, most souls search for their life's meaning throughout their lifetime. Every step of the way, the universe is helping us realize our soul's genius and the lessons it imparts to us. From my amateur golf career to being a wife and mother, to being a business owner, I felt a calling deep within my soul to express my authentic self. I love business, being a visionary, embarking on new horizons and contributing to the world around me.

As I shared with you, I spent over a decade volunteering and working on several different business ventures. Several of my business projects were hugely successful, but then failed to weather the storm of the Great Recession of 2009. I had worked extremely hard to achieve what we had achieved, only to be sent down a slippery slope of financial loss and heartache. It was one of the lowest times in my life. I had allowed my sense of well-being to be contingent upon my external world, where my successes and failures defined me. For months, I failed to live in a place of love, balance and harmony. Then, I realized that I had to give myself love and forgiveness in order to move on.

Five years later, Jenna passed away. Again, had I not learned to be in touch with our infinite nature, the external storm and magnitude of such a horrific loss could have wreaked havoc upon me for the rest of my life. I built upon all that I had learned in the years prior. Unlike my experience in 2009, I allowed myself right away to align with the love of everything and everyone around me. I no longer had an egocentric agenda. I now understood that the world didn't owe me anything. All I could think about was how I could express my love for my daughter and the world around me. Through this understanding, Jenna's life and death have had an amazing impact on my soul's growth and a beautiful impact on the world.

Life's circumstances provide us with the catalyst and motivation to peel back the layers that shroud our soul's purpose. Throughout my life, I have been given many opportunities to learn and practice resiliency, acceptance and forgiveness. It is important to stay the course and understand that we are here for a beautiful and loving reason, even though at times it feels quite the opposite. Just like Adele, we have poetic lyrics to write and beautiful songs to sing. We can learn that we are more than a word, more than a note, and more than an instrument. We are more than our successes, our failures, our losses. It means that, when we understand the beauty of what we are, we will create all that divinity calls us to be and do.

Teacher's Aids

Parents, teachers and coaches are among those who have a special role in the development of another's soul. Being able to devote yourself to such pursuits is an extremely special gift. Such teachers also reside in the non-physical realm. We call them spirit guides. They are responsible for helping us fulfill the spiritual contract we made with ourselves before we incarnated to the physical world. When it's time, divine time, for our spirit guides to help us, they tune in to our energy and help direct us to fulfill our destiny.

Just what is a spiritual contract? If we believe that we are spiritual beings having a human experience, it seems reasonable to expect a blueprint or plan for us to follow, before we enter a human body. That blueprint includes the landscape and circumstances in which we enter the physical world. On a soul level, we grasp that this includes the parents we choose, our socio-economic level, our gifts and our physical surroundings. They also serve as guides or lesson plans for what we want to learn during a given lifespan. As spiritual beings, we want to learn and grow by choosing different experiences. As we learn from our human experiences, we evolve as energetic beings. Over many lifetimes, we attempt to know ourselves and understand our connection and oneness with our divinity and find the balance and harmony within our shared energy.

While we are between lifetimes, our spirit guides help us to reflect on things we would like to learn and better understand in order to raise the vibrational energy of our soul. For example, as we review our previous incarnations, we may determine that we want or need to learn more about compassion, humility or contribution. We may focus on one or several lessons at each stage. The goal of each lesson is to balance our energy through love, compassion and kindness.

The frustrating, yet humorous aspect of soul contracts is that we're unable to remember them once we are born. At times this leaves us feeling a sense of separateness from the whole, of being completely alone. Consciously working on ourselves and becoming aware of our connection to the love and light of our Creator make the human experience quite rewarding, despite its inherent challenges.

This reminds me of my college days, when I would study for hours and hours for a big exam and then be elated when I would ace the test. That's how life is. Studying can be difficult, and subjects can pose great challenges. Some lessons are easier to grasp than others. We may need to repeat some of them for a deeper, richer understanding. When we experience success through our efforts and tenacity, we begin to see the potential that lies within us. The experience is awe-inspiring.

Even though souls enter into prearranged contracts, we have free will once we incarnate. Sadly, many souls choose not to learn their lessons in a given lifetime, due to the harsh climate surrounding their physical and emotional experience. Instead, they check out and live their lives in pain and despair. Don't get me wrong, I completely understand. The conditions and emotions of life can be harsh. I often pray that I have the strength to learn the arduous lessons I set out to learn. But, if you're like me, you're thinking, "Why sign up for the class in the first place?" I have asked myself this question many times. What makes a soul enter into a negative experience, like an abusive childhood or a cruel relationship? The answer is simple. Sometimes you learn the most from the toughest teachers.

I remember agreeing to run a marathon as a way of testing my internal strength and bring attention to #hersmile's efforts. I trained for months. My seasonal allergies kicked in two months before the event, rendering me temporarily asthmatic. I was determined to run the race, even though my condition compromised my training. On the day of the race, I ran the first thirteen miles pretty easily. The last thirteen were grueling. My knees began to lock up and my hands began to swell.

I thought about cheating, turning around and heading back to the finish line. Challenging thoughts surfaced. "Who the hell needs to do this anyway? Do you know you're crazy for thinking you could do this? You didn't even train properly." I wanted to quit so badly, but the amazing thing is, I didn't. I dug deep within myself and remembered why I chose to do the race in the first place. Setting out for a challenge is completely different from the act of doing it. Once your soul creates a blueprint for the lessons it is setting out to master when it incarnates, it may underestimate how extremely difficult it is to persevere, when we are in the physical realm. Nonetheless, our soul and our guides knew in advance that we could handle it. And, once we embrace the challenging journey we created for ourselves, our human experience will forever be altered—for the better.

Calling All Spirit Guides

Wouldn't it be so much easier if we could call, email or text our spirit guides? For some, that instant connection is how it works. It just takes time and practice to be able to hear, see, or feel our guides.

During one of my early visits with my grief counselor, Kathryn Davi Cardinale, she handed me a copy of her book, *Joseph, My Son—My Guide: Communication From the Baby I Lost at Birth, A True Story*. I looked at her in disbelief, "What?" I said, "You wrote this book?" She nodded. Inside, she had written: "Dena and Paul, trust your inner guidance and believe Jenna is near. Love, Kathryn."

I devoured Kathryn's words in a day. I learned that in the late 1950s she was the mother of two healthy children. Her third child was stillborn, a baby girl she named Mary Ann. A year later, her fourth pregnancy had complications and the doctor had to induce labor. The baby, a little boy named Joseph, survived only three minutes. Kathryn then had a fifth baby named Anthony. Again, she had major complications with the pregnancy. He lived only five-and-a-half hours.

Kathryn underwent a hysterectomy after her fifth pregnancy. Through her own experiences with loss, she became a certified grief counselor and clinical hypnotherapist. She volunteered her time to those struggling with the grief of a loved one's passing. Her book is not about grief. Instead, she shares the miracle of reconnection and messages, both personal and universal; messages delivered by her spirit guide, Joseph, her fourth son.

A friend had introduced Kathryn to automatic writing in 1983. Her first experience left her feeling strange and apprehensive. Since that time, the communication and spirit energy Joseph imparted has increasingly and consistently moved through her. In 1999, Kathryn reached out to Kay Taylor, a nationally recognized intuitive guide in Taos, New Mexico. Kathryn asked if she could tell her anything about the name Joseph and that she had sensed that he may be her spirit guide.

"Kay was quiet for a few moments," Kathryn said, "tapping into her own guidance."

"Yes, that is the child. He is your guide. He is a partner in the grief work you do. He is a very light being. He was guiding you even before he connected to the body and has continued working with you. Your inspiration comes from him. He draws specific people to you. You have communicated with him for so long that you don't recognize the difference." Kay urged her to reach out to him.

"I can't believe a baby I gave birth to many years ago is my guide. This is exciting!" Kathryn had replied that night at bedtime, gratefully calling to her son, "Well, Joseph, I guess we're a team."

Over the next decade, Kathryn transcribed a complete manuscript. The profound message in her writing revealed: "My wish for you is that these messages will inspire you to listen to your inner voice. You are here for a reason. You are significant. Embrace the wonderful spiritual being that you are, and EXPECT MIRACLES!"

Kathryn's moving experiences inspired me to start journaling and connecting to spirit.

You Are Truly Never Alone

Wouldn't it be great if your guides could simply call you on the phone and tell you what's coming in your future, to brace for the storm ahead, or that your child needs you, and you should get to them right away? For some people, that's how it works. It just takes time and practice to hear, see or feel our guides.

After reading Kathryn's book, I asked her to teach me more about automatic writing. She explained the process in very simple terms, as I'm going to do for you. She told me to go to a peaceful setting, either inside my home or out in nature. Open to a page in my journal and begin writing whatever is on my mind at that moment. I wish I had learned to connect years ago.

Continue to write until your mind begins to relax. As you enter a meditative-like state, write, "Only the love and light of our Creator may come through to me. Spirits not of the light are unwelcome here." Hold the pen lightly to the paper and then ask spirit a question. Write whatever words come to you. Keep going as if you're having a conversation. It may seem like you're forming the words from your imagination, but you'll soon realize the words are being dictated to you. They are not your own voice. Yes, it's that magical.

I began to journal several weeks after Jenna died. It felt good to write out all the emotions I was harboring. My heart ached. I longed to create a path of healing for my family. I already had so many gifts from Jenna, but this time I looked for signs. I cherished each one, but they weren't enough for me to work through my myriad emotions. The following are some of my initial entries.

May 19, 2014

It has been several days since I've written. I am working on Julia's room (a room which had been our play room). The drywall man came on

135

Saturday and today I'm going to paint the ceiling and prime the walls. I'm looking forward to making the space hers. I walked Briones this morning and then talked to Mom. I must continue to give love and maintain balance. Only the love and light of our Creator may come through to me. Other spirits that are not of the light are unwelcome here. Do you have a message for me?

Look inside yourself. The message and the way are already there. It is safe within you. You are powerful, more than you know. Do you know why I came to you?

All I know is I love you and knew you had a magical ability to draw people to you. When you loved someone, you truly loved and cared about them. You were very easy to forgive, too. You cared and had great work ethic. I'm not sure if you brought people together, or if they came together simply because of who you are. So why is it you came to me?

I came to you so you could lead people. So, you could show people what is possible. You are on the right path. Continue to write to me and I will guide you. You have much to do. Getting your affairs in order is important. Your mind must not be burdened.

What about working?

You will have abundance. God will not forsake you for doing your work.

Thank you for letting me know that I am on the right track. Will you give me a sign in the clouds? I look for you there.

Yes. (heart symbol)

May 20, 2014

Yesterday was truly a magical day. I asked you for a sign in the clouds that you were with me. When I left the cemetery, I looked for signs everywhere in the sky, but there were no noticeable signs of you. I ran some errands and continued to look for you. About an hour and a half later, I went to Home Depot. When I came out to my car to put the paint supplies away, I looked up to the clouds, but there were no signs of you. Then as I went to close the rear hatch of our car, I looked over my right shoulder up to the sky. I was amazed at what I saw. It was the most beautiful rainbow. It wasn't a normal rainbow that arches from one side of the horizon to the other. It was much smaller and way high in the sky. It was shaped like a smile and was of the most vibrant colors with pink/red on top. It moved me to tears. I want to thank you with all my heart and soul for such a magical and amazing gift. I want you to know how much I love you. What a gift all my children have been to me. I pray you will show me the way. I pray to you that you will help make our small portion of the world better than when we found it. I pray we represent the greatest of possibilities. When I look out upon the cemetery, I'm struck with the question, "Did all these souls make a difference?" Only the love and light of our Creator may come through to me. Any spirits who are not of the light are unwelcome here. Who is with me now?

Many are with you now. You have much to do. Stay calm. Calm your mind. Stay attuned to the signs all around you. You will bring people together for goodness.

Should I continue to write?

Writing is good. It helps you connect with us.

Is Jenna with you? Where is Jenna today?

She is all around you.

Why does she not speak with me today?

Today is not the day.

Will she speak with me again?

Yes.

This entry holds a very special place in my heart, for it is the first time I asked for a specific sign via my writing. In this case, it was a sign in the clouds and it was granted. During my May 19th journal entry, I spoke with Jenna. I could feel her and had a knowing that it was her. Then, there was the amazing sight of the small rainbow in the sky. It did not rain in Northern California that day. In fact, we were in the midst of several years of drought. Yet, high in the sky was a magnificent rainbow. What is hard to communicate about signs is that they come paired with a feeling, a knowingness that you can't quite put into words. You just know the sign was meant for you!

Soul's Purpose

Very few people walk this Earth knowing their purpose. For the few, their purpose may appear through their God-given gifts, their academic aptitude or their worldly wisdom. But, those people are the minority, which leaves most souls trying to answer the question, "Why am I here?"

Many people pursue specific avenues in life and spend years honing a skill only to feel unclear and oftentimes lost or unfulfilled. Prior to Jenna's passing, I continued to fill my days searching for something I knew was inside me. Aside from the utter love I had for my family, I sensed that my authentic self was not being fulfilled. I found clues as to what made my heart sing, but unfortunately I didn't have strong inner guidance from any spiritual practices to discover my soul's true purpose.

Through Jenna's passing, I've learned that each soul has a unique path. To serve your soul's true purpose, it's important to be faithful to your path. It's through this courageous act that your soul's journey experiences its own blessings of growth. And, in the most beautiful way, it impacts others as well. I learned this lesson during one of my early writings.

July 8, 2014

From feathers to butterflies, to hummingbirds, to feeling like you've kissed me goodnight, every sign has been so meaningful. So beautiful. I've been thinking so much about what I call the riddle of why we came to this Earthly experience. Why did you pick us as your parents? How did that help your soul's journey? You challenged me. You forced me to look at myself as a parent, commit to becoming a better person. You were a joy, smart, you had a hard work ethic, artistic, sensitive, resilient, tough, loyal, silly, fun and beautiful inside and out. You were a great sister, granddaughter, etc. So, with all that said, why are we all connected? Now, I can only think about keeping your spirit alive and contributing to the world. I feel something big inside me. But what is it? What is my soul's journey? How are we all related? How are your sisters' souls related and affected by our loss of you? What about daddy? I pray to be graced by God's white light and to learn and contribute. What does my soul need to do in this life? I pray all those who have loved and who have passed will guide me to a higher purpose. Only the love and light of our Creator may come through to me. No other spirits that are not of the light are welcome here. Who is with me now?

Know we are with you and we shall guide you. Continue on your path. You are on the right path. You have learned to open up your soul more than ever before. You will show people the way and how to be. People will continue to be attracted to you. You will do all things for good. Do not worry about resources. They will be given to you.

Who is my guide?

I am here with you. I have always been here with you. You have taken my path for you well in this life. You were right to think that people have to overcome their own hardship.

So, what shall I focus on?

#hersmile. That will open up every door for you.

What will #hersmile allow us to do?

It will allow you to do business with a purpose. Your purpose is what the journey is all about.

What is the purpose?

Dig deep in to your soul. You already know. Be the change you want to see in the world.

What should I do to understand my purpose? I still feel unclear.

Continue to write daily for one year. It will all come to you.

I continued to write and spirit continued to come. I began to grow beyond my physical body and mind. One time I asked how I could have a deeper connection with spirit, Jenna, and my loved ones. Through spirit I wrote, *"You have a connection deep within you. Everyone has it."* I went on to ask how we could find the connection. Spirit answered, *"It's in stillness. It's in letting go."* I was confused and queried, *"Letting go of what?"* Spirit explained that I must let go of tangible items because of the obstacles they present. Spirit continued, *"It's in stillness where your life's purpose lies. When you spend your days wanting, when the desire is influenced from outside your true self, it is there then, when you are lost."*

Calling All Signs

As my spiritual journey has unfolded, I have learned that there are signs and help all around us. They don't come only in the form of writing. Remember, you are here for a specific soul purpose, a purpose that no one else can fulfill. Your spirit guides want to help you on your path. Discovering and then understanding and living your soul's purpose are part of a process that unfolds along different timelines for different people. Everything happens in its own divine time. So, be patient and commit to being a loving being. At times you may fail, but continue on the path anyway. As your awareness grows and expands, you will find greater opportunities for realizing your life's purpose.

Before I outline other signs, how will you know you're not just imagining them? You'll know according to the messages and signs that come your way. Spirit that is of the light and love of our Creator always wants the best for you. Some lessons may hurt, but in the end, life's challenges make you more loving, understanding, kind and compassionate. You will recognize the voice that is coming to you as not your own and you'll feel like the words, thoughts or images are being dictated to you. The words are never judgmental, unsupportive or harsh. After interacting with spirit through my writing, I often find myself tired, yet feeling truly peaceful. A lot of high vibrational energy is exchanged, when you transfer information with spirit. Don't be surprised if it wears you out.

Sending Signs

Upon Jenna's passing, I received many signs, but one of my favorites was when feathers suddenly appeared in our house and around me. One day, I was at Starbucks speaking to a mom about Jenna, our moving forward, and the enormity of love I felt for her. Once I got on the topic of love, a feather floated down from the ceiling and hovered around my face at eye level. It stayed there for the longest time and I was truly amazed and in disbelief. That continues to happen to me when I talk about love. I'll just stop for a moment and thank Jenna and spirit for acknowledging that I'm on the right track.

Guides can also coordinate your running into someone or seeing something that can help you on your journey. I'm confident my spirit guides brought my husband back into my life, because we were destined to be together. I thank them with all my heart for leading me to the man who completes me. So, pay attention to things that repeat themselves in your life. Someone is trying to give you a message.

Communication can also arise from your intuition, from the people being sent into your life, from your gut feelings, or from your dreams at night. The more you open yourself up to the signs that already exist all around you, the more awareness and clarity you'll have of your life's purpose. It's a good idea to write down the signs you experience during the week. Remember, when you beckon your spirit guides, to also say that only those of the love and light of our Creator are welcome. You don't need any mischievous spirits in your space.

Misconceptions of Meditation

Most people view meditation as a monastic practice that calls for completely turning off your thoughts. For monks and those leading a life of solitude, this may be a suitable goal, but for people like you and me, it's not even close to realistic. Never feel like you've failed, if you attempt to meditate and cannot turn off your thoughts. That shouldn't be your goal anyway. Instead, use meditation as a means to set aside time to guide your thoughts and gain an intimate glimpse into your mind and yourself. You can start meditating just a few minutes a day. Only increase the time once you start seeing its benefits in your life. Remember, it's a non-chaotic time set aside to guide your mind and come in touch with the thoughts you entertain on a regular basis. It's a quiet time, yet a dynamic process. Your goal isn't to have a blank slate; it is to lightly guide your mind toward a greater awareness of what thoughts permeate your being. You can also invite your spirit guides into this quiet space and ask them for direction. Stay aware of the images and voices that come through you that are not yours. Through a heightened consciousness, you can better guide your day-to-day choices. In time, your connection will become stronger, and the information you get will be more accurate and applicable to your life.

Discovering clues to identifying your life's purpose is an interactive process. Unfortunately, your spirit guides aren't going to send you an email or text, pointing you in the direction of deeper understanding of why challenges exist in your life. You must ask the questions, be extremely patient, and then look for the signs leading you to understand and live out your soul's purpose. As for my own journey, everything I experienced for more than three decades led me to write this book and start a nonprofit to help those forced to bear the unbearable loss of a loved one. It's important to stay the course and let divine time unfold—although it can be frustrating. You may feel as though you are not fulfilling your true purpose. Just remember that there is a season and reason for everything. Your soul and your spirit guides are communicating with you all the time. Their greatest aspiration is for you to fulfill your soul's destiny.

Chapter 9

Tools in the Toolbox

Doing your soul's work isn't an easy process. It takes courage to move forward with a life of great intention. And one must be courageous to embark on a journey of awareness and self-reflection. Yet, how can you focus on all that you are, when your true self is marred by your life's experiences, the world around you, and your belief system? You can. You simply need the tools to do so.

It's no surprise that we live in a time of instant gratification, as social media, the media, and the entertainment industry are shaping people's identities. A picture posted on social media can create the illusion that a person is doing great. What it doesn't show is the person dying inside. Those images tell very little about our shared challenges and our life's true purpose. We struggle to be unique and different. We try to hide behind the backdrop of a beautiful home, our child's stellar report card, or toasting glasses of champagne, but rest assured that not doing your soul's work will leave you feeling lost and empty inside. Culturally, we are taught to look out for "number one" and do anything we can to compete our way to the top. We give trophies to every child, because we don't want hurt feelings. This framework gives us very few tools to process and cope with life's challenges.

Those who have overcome adversity and live a life of joy, peace and intention have not done so through our cultural teachings of selfishness, blame, entitlement or victimization, but through compassion, kindness and contribution. It's in connectedness and recognition of the soul's abundance that true resiliency lies. They afford you the opportunity to create an internal world of balance and hope, despite your circumstances. Tools allow the sculptor to make their vision a reality. Michelangelo said, "I saw the angel in the marble and carved until I set him free." To experience the power and beauty that lie within your soul, you must be willing to try on another pair of lenses, see things differently, ask different questions, incorporate more powerful beliefs, and be willing to accept the beauty of who you are.

Why Does Resiliency Matter?

On April 20, 1999, two teens went on a shooting spree at Columbine High School in Littleton, Colorado, killing 13 people and wounding more than 20 others, before turning their guns on themselves and completing suicide. Since then, the U.S. has endured more than 50 mass shootings. That's screaming evidence that, in our culture, we aren't doing a good enough job teaching behavioral health, resiliency and coping skills.

As I shared with you earlier, I had many tools to call upon after Jenna's passing. I had spent many years developing them through my family experience and my pursuit of becoming a professional golfer. I took classes, read books, and became a student of the power of mindset. Were it not for the tools in my toolbox, I'm not sure where I would be today.

We are all born with the *capability* to be resilient, but our *capacity* to be resilient is entirely different. We must learn to bounce back in the face of stress, trauma or tragedy by utilizing strategies that tap into the essence of our soul and not into our egocentric selves. The result of not learning these skills is to continue to be faced with mass killings in our country, bullying in our schools, hazing in our sports, colleges and workplace, and our

150

own darkness and devastation when personal trauma and tragedy strike.

To build resiliency tools, we must first explore the essence of the soul.

Soul Sense

As theologian George MacDonald said, "You don't have a soul. You are a Soul. You have a body." The essence of who we are is our soul. Each soul is not a separate being but instead is a piece of the whole. Therefore, what each soul needs in order to cope with the harshness of the human experience is the same. In the same way that our soul resides within the external capsule of our physical body, we need both internal and external tools to foster resiliency. All are rooted in unconditional love and include connection, compassion, kindness, awareness, and intention.

I know firsthand how difficult it is to model all these soul attributes. It takes practice. Our emotions, attitudes and stress reactions affect our entire system. Utilizing the following tools on a regular basis will help you find a sense of purpose and belief in a bright future, despite your circumstances. Just remember, you have an abundance of gifts to give yourself and the world around you.

151

Connection

A good friend of mine, Mara, lost her daughter shortly after Jenna passed away. Many months after her daughter's death, a friend of hers reached out to her on Facebook and asked if she'd like to go to lunch. Mara accepted her invitation, but the friend never followed up. One day, Mara was at the grocery store when she saw her friend down the aisle. The woman pretended not to see her, but Mara greeted her anyway. The awkward exchange left Mara feeling hurt and perplexed. "What did I do to her? Why would she invite me to lunch and then totally ignore me?"

Many people are averse to walking side-by-side with someone in emotional pain. They fear not knowing the right thing to say and putting themselves in an emotionally vulnerable state. With the right tools, you can help people help you. Of course, while you're processing the shock of your loss and coping with your grief, you may feel that helping others help you is the last thing you want to undertake. I understand. Still, some simple tools will help in this area. They might not work on every one of your friendships or acquaintances, but the following are sure to work on many associations and will help you feel a greater sense of connection.

Connection & Independence

My mom often told me she was raising me to be independent and self-reliant. Yet, when Jenna died, I went against the grain and purposely tried not to be self-sufficient. I shared my grief with our family, friends and community. Jenna wasn't just mine, she was all of ours, and together we bonded over our loss. This meant allowing people to do things that I once would have had too much pride to concede. I surrendered. And, their love lifted us up in unimaginable ways.

In "A Time to Grieve," Kenneth C. Haugk writes: "God never intended us to suffer alone. He created us to care for and support others in their time of need – and to allow others to care for and support us in ours. This is being *inter-dependent*, which is God's original plan, rather than independent, which can be a very lonely way to grieve."

In Mara's case, the fact that her friend left her feeling hurt and unloved called for her to rely upon tools she already had in her toolbox. Mara felt *empathy* toward her friend and understood the challenges this woman must have been facing within her own heart that weren't allowing her to be in Mara's vulnerable space.

She also called upon her sense of *responsiveness* by becoming a speaker for a national organization, which allowed her to share her daughter's story with others. Reaching out helped her feel deeply connected inside. As St. Francis of Assisi said, "For it is in giving that we receive."

Another means to help you feel connected is *communication.* It has many facets, but one of the first building blocks is how we communicate with our higher self. Asking such insightful questions as, "What actions do I need to take to get through this moment in an uplifting way?" or "How can I share my love for my loved one today?" Empowering questions lead to empowering answers. If we continually find ourselves in a dark space, we need to pay close attention to how we talk to ourselves and to the questions we are asking.

Talking with another person or affiliating with a group empowers and supports us, giving us a sense of connection. We may need to reach beyond our friends and family to find such support, and that's completely OKAY!

We may be reluctant to communicate our needs to those around us, as we struggle to navigate the pain and grief we are experiencing. However, consideration is a two-way street. Being able to communicate our needs, pain and hurt feelings is key.

Connection comes in many forms. Some tools to add to our toolbox are interdependence, empathy, responsiveness and communication. Expecting the world around us to respond in a time of need can potentially set us up for disappointment. We need to be what we want to attract in life. If we do this, we will feel connected beyond riches.

Compassion

It was the Sunday evening after Christmas. Paul and I were watching *60 Minutes*. I was deep in thought when a woman, whom I'll call Kelly, came into my mind. Her daughter passed away in the beginning of 2015. Her death was completely unexpected and left her family understandably broken. As it turned out, we shared two mutual friends and both had recommended that Kelly contact me to share what she was going through with someone who might better understand. She reached out via text. She said she thought she might be ready to speak with other people who had experienced similar losses. I responded that I would love to speak with her when the time felt right to her. She ended up calling me right away, and we connected through the loss of our beautiful daughters. In the months that followed, we spoke on the phone a few times and texted back and forth on occasion. On that Sunday night, I thought about how her Christmas was and reflected on how difficult the 'first' of everything is when you go through it without your child or loved one by your side. So, I texted a simple message: "Thinking of you."

What she wrote back was heartbreaking. She shared that I had deeply hurt her by not including her family in our holiday card outreach from our #hersmile Nonprofit and that she thought I would have greater consideration for her. She said there were no second chances.

My heart raced. Had I failed her? I never meant to hurt her or leave her out. I thought I was speaking to her as a fellow grieving mother and that our connection was separate from #hersmile because we met under different circumstances.

I texted her back, trying to explain and understand her point of view but I only seemed to make matters worse. The pain and anger of her grief were blaring.

I sat in disbelief. The sadness subsided. I knew I needed to learn from this. My thoughts were agitated and ran rapid within me. I declared, "All I can do is have my experiences make me better and not bitter, as I have chosen to do with every facet of my life, and this will be no different. I will learn from this and I will be more aware of what people expect from me. I understand that I did not intentionally try to hurt anyone and that people project their pain out into the world when they are suffering so desperately."

So that was it. I had spoken my truth. I never meant to hurt her and I learned a huge life lesson. Only when you have *compassion* for another's heartache and pain is it possible not to take their words as a personal attack. Although my first reaction was sadness, I used *critical thinking* as a tool in realizing that love means wanting the best for someone, even if your relationship fails. It means when you love one being, you love all beings. Souls are not separate from the whole; they make up the whole. Compassion means always keeping the door to your heart open, which means the door will also be open to you as well. Only when we offer compassion to another do we know what it means to give it to ourselves.

Kindness

Wouldn't it be great if we all treated one another the way we want to be treated? When embroiled in the whirlwind of our own emotions, we often become reactive instead of proactive. Kindness finds its roots in friendliness, generosity and consideration. Yet, when riddled with emotional pain, anger and suffering, we may

157

feel averse to the notion of being kind, not only to others but also to ourselves. Our expectations may be unrealistic or not communicated, leaving us struggling to figure out why people aren't giving us what we need.

It is important to have tools that help you project the kindness that resides within you, so you can in turn attract kindness. Skills such as *listening*, *understanding* and *communicating* are vital to moving toward a life of peace.

Kindness and Expectations

About a year and a half after Jenna passed away, I received a text from one of my very best friends. I'll call her Shelly. She included a link to a CNN article, "Inside the Secret World of Teens," about their addiction to their cell phones, specifically their addiction to smartphones and social media. I found myself feeling more and more hurt. I said quietly to myself, "Doesn't she know I lost my daughter because she risked her life to retrieve her cell phone from the train tracks? Doesn't she understand that I know all too well the addiction our kids have to social media and their phones?" I thought better of texting her back, considering my heightened emotions. I told myself to wait until morning to see how I felt then.

In the morning, I was still upset that she had sent that article to me. I expected her to be more sensitive and considerate of my feelings. Maybe she just didn't care or, better yet, maybe she just didn't get how difficult this journey is. I texted her, "What made you send this to me?"

She called me and said, "Why wouldn't I send it to you? I sent it to everyone I know who has a teenager." Now angry and hurt, I burst. Kindness was the farthest thing from my mind at that moment. "You just don't get it, do you?" I said. "Don't you think we know all too well the dangers of cells phones? I don't think you get this journey we've been thrust upon?" My rant was cut short. She began to cry and said she had to get off the phone.

We barely spoke for months.

It was the second week of the New Year when Shelly called me. The conversation started off with small talk, but I couldn't take it any longer. Not having cleared the air with her for months was blocking me from having a full relationship with her. "Are we moving forward and trying to brush everything under the rug from the situation we had months ago?" I said. She still didn't understand what upset me so much. I understood that she was just trying to be helpful. She's against giving her 12-

year-old a cell phone and is critical of others who make that choice. We weren't making much headway. I arrived at my appointment and had to go. We agreed to finish the conversation later.

I had the rest of the day to think about how I could honor and understand her feelings, be kind and help her understand and honor mine. The next morning, I called and told her I had time to think about our conversation from the day before. "I'm not trying to make you wrong. I'm hoping I can help you understand that your words really hurt me and why. I guess the bottom line is I do have expectations of you. Maybe I shouldn't. You are one of my oldest and closest friends. We've been through so much together. I try not to expect any special treatment from anyone. I don't want you to feel sorry for me, but I think I do expect you to have a level of sensitivity and consideration towards Jenna's passing," I said this as calmly as I could.

She replied, "I try to be there for you, but when I ask you how you are and you say fine, I assume you don't want to talk, so I don't push it. You know I think about you every day."

As the conversation continued, we began to bridge the gap in our understanding of one another. What I said next finally made the connection. "You love animals. What if one day your outdoor animal was hit and killed by a car, then shortly thereafter I sent you an article about the risk involved in letting your domestic animals live outdoors? It's not that the information wasn't meant to be helpful; it's just that the pain in your heart over losing your pet is still so intense. Does that make sense?"

She said she totally got it and apologized.

It had been more than a year and a half since I received that text from Shelly, but the pain of losing Jenna was still raw. I never realized until that point that I had expectations of the people in my close inner circle. As hard as I try to be kind, gracious and strong, I'm now aware that I have a great vulnerability inside myself.

One of the greatest tools we have is our taking *responsibility* for how we interact and what we expect from others. Also, when we seek to *understand* one another, it doesn't necessarily mean we agree. This realization was a huge 'aha' moment for me. Seeking to understand someone's perspective means you offer the kindness and graciousness necessary to truly listen to what's in her heart and try to understand what she does or thinks. It took me months of hurt feelings to finally step outside of my expectations and seek to understand

161

Shelly. I began to understand that she never meant to hurt me, and my interpretation of her actions was embedded in my own pain. Remember, it's everyone's default to see life through his or her own lenses and belief systems. Trying on someone else's lens takes strong intention. I know from firsthand experience that seeking to understand another person and taking the time to communicate our needs takes a lot of energy. At that moment, we may feel we just don't have the energy to give. This is to be expected.

So, please, be kind to yourself. Also, be kind to those around you. Be willing to tell the people in your life that you may need time to understand your own feelings and vulnerabilities, before you can help them understand what you need. By seeking to understand them and by keeping your lines of communication open, you will continue to draw love and support into your life and be able to release with love those who are unable to give you what you need.

Awareness

Self-awareness and self-reflection are ongoing. However, devoting *time* to increasing awareness allows us to peel back the layers of our self and understand that the conversations and images we entertain are a direct result of how we define ourselves and our life's circumstances. Mastery of self is extremely difficult. Our emotions can make it difficult to navigate the physical world. In fact, we're hardwired to seek safety within our environment at all times. Life's traumas leave many of us lost, insecure and held hostage by the shackles of our own negative thoughts and emotions. Our traumatic memories are stored deep within us. Although we can recall or stifle our memories, it's hard to shut off the emotional and physical response that memories have over our being and, consequently, over our lives. Many people adopt self-destructive behaviors as a direct result of not becoming aware of the impact trauma has in their lives. Emotional response to trauma directly influences our nervous system. Negative emotions can trigger fear, depression, anxiety and insecurities that, in turn, create stress. We are left wondering how we ended up feeling so lost. Awareness allows us to recognize the pain within you and simply sit with it. It affords us the opportunity to recognize it and assess what continues to give life to our emotional suffering and what exacerbates it. Since human beings are hardwired to seek safety, it's no wonder that the pain and traumas of our lives leave an indelible mark upon us. The human psyche wants to avoid pain and does its best to chronicle what causes it.

However, the paradox is this: the only way to emotional safety is to work through our pain and traumas by becoming aware of their existence within us. I often say, "The only way through the pain is to feel the pain," meaning, don't avoid the pain that resides within you. Acknowledge its existence and it will dissipate or, at least, lessen its stranglehold over us.

As we continue to sharpen our awareness tool through different forms of meditating, writing, art and/or communicating with positive influences in our life, a metamorphosis starts to take shape. This takes time and intention, and we need to take one moment at a time.

As each moment passes through you, be aware of your breath; perhaps you will feel your heartbeat. You will begin to hear the inner voice that makes up your thoughts. Images will flash inside your mind. You will realize how your emotional internalization and/or emotional response to the traumas you have experienced have shaped you.

It's important to remember that you are not broken. You are a soul living the human experience. The landscape can be extremely harsh. Having an emotional response to life is to be expected. That's how the soul's understanding of itself grows.

Self-Mastery Is a Process

I don't think mental and emotional traumas ever truly leave us. One evening, my husband Paul was watching sports on TV and chatting with a friend on the phone. He told his buddy he had to go, because he wanted to pick up Julia from practice. We caught each other's eye and he waved good-bye. A few seconds later, he said, "Dena, I feel really dizzy." I told him to come back and sit down. Thinking he might be dehydrated, I gave him water and another drink for his electrolytes and offered to get Julia.

I called him several minutes later. He answered, but he didn't sound good, telling me he felt nauseous and was vomiting. I was anxious to get home. The trip to pick up Julia seemed considerably longer than normal. I called Paul two more times. He was still vomiting. I was scared.

Finally home, I hurried upstairs to find Paul retching over the toilet. He hadn't stopped vomiting. I called the advice nurse, explained Paul's condition, and she advised me to get him to the ER. I called our neighbors and good friends to help. Clyde helped get Paul in the car and the girls, now both home, went to stay with them. The girls were noticeably upset. What I wasn't showing on the outside was my inner turmoil. I understood the impact this was having on the girls and myself. Your mind doesn't forget trauma; it just finds ways to deal with it.

The ER is less than 15 minutes away. The entire time, all I could do was pray that Paul wouldn't die. I understand those are extreme thoughts, but once someone gets suddenly swept away from you, your mind doesn't forget. Paul was diagnosed with vertigo. Many hours later, he was sent home with a good prognosis, but it would take him time to recover. For me, well, it would take time to heal in an entirely different way.

As family members expressed their concerns, they also started telling us what to do. Rationally, I knew everyone was concerned, and of course all they wanted to do was help, but emotionally I felt like they were questioning my ability to advocate for my own husband. "Do this. Ask that. Why didn't they do this or that? Take him to a specialist." On and on they continued. I was no longer petrified that I would lose Paul. I felt angry now. I couldn't help but think crazy thoughts, such as, "Do they think I can't take care of Paul, because I couldn't keep Jenna safe?" Thoughts like that ran rampant as my anger grew. At one point someone said, "What if he was driving when this happened?" I belted out, "Then I guess he would have died and I don't really want to think about that." I wasn't in a good place. I felt like I was going to explode.

After Paul's trip to the ER, another layer of self-awareness surfaced. It was clear that I still had a lot of healing to do. I'm beginning to understand that when you experience grief and trauma in your life, they take up residency. Grieving and trauma in our lives doesn't have a start and finish, and it doesn't come with a road map. The trip to the ER taught me that I will continue to emotionally stumble and fall along this journey and that with every imperfection comes the gift of awareness. Just as the doctor had used tools to diagnose Paul's vertigo, I now know I need more coping tools to call on the next time a crisis hits our family.

Two of the greatest tools for building awareness are *acknowledging* your emotions and taking *responsibility* for them. After I knew Paul was going to be okay, anger washed over me. I wasn't angry at those trying to help us. I was angry that I feared losing another person in my life. I was angry that even with all the positive strides we, as a family, had made over the last two years, there were no guarantees that our foundation could not be rocked again. And I was angry that I questioned whether people trusted that I could take care of Paul. After days of stewing, I stopped adding fuel to the fire. I began simply to notice my thoughts. I listened to the internal conversation.

I have found the best way for me to become aware of my thoughts is to meditate or talk to someone I trust and respect. By meditating and practicing simple breathing techniques, the chatter in your mind becomes easier and easier to decipher. As you notice your thoughts, do not judge them. Simply notice them. Remember, it is through awareness that dissipation comes.

Intention—The Final Frontier

I have learned that the only way through trauma and pain is to be *aware* of my emotional response to them. No one goes through life intending to face such stressful emotions. On the contrary, most of us do everything we can to avoid pain. Our ability to recognize, direct, and positively express our emotions is what allows us to overcome life's traumas and challenges and live lives of intention, despite our circumstances.

Understanding our emotions takes time. The best news is that it's definitely a skill we can learn and hone. As we become aware of the assumptions and conclusions we have made about life, our relationship to it, our physical response, and the questions we ask ourselves, we become better able to understand that the one thing

168

we are in charge of is our emotional response to life's circumstances. *Once we truly get this, we can begin to direct our lives with a degree of intention we may not have thought possible.*

People react differently to trauma, but we all experience emotional and physical pain. Both are located and activated in the same area of the brain. Emotional responses to trauma may invoke feelings of shock, depression, anger, anxiety, loneliness, and/or being misunderstood. Common physiological responses to loss of a loved one include the painful sensation of a broken heart, with a corresponding imbalance between heart rate and respiration, and activating the sympathetic nervous system's 'fight or flight' response.

As I watched the paramedics working on Jenna's body and the reality of her fate washed over me, my emotional shock took over my physical being. I shook uncontrollably. I'll never forget my emotional and physical response to Jenna's passing. The connection between the two cannot be denied. My gut rumbled. I felt nauseous. I remember telling myself to breathe . . . just breathe.

Understanding the connection between your emotions and your physical well-being can be life changing. Although there's no right or wrong way to think, feel or respond to trauma in your life, *guiding your emotions* with the intention of finding powerful meaning cannot be stressed enough.

Having the intention and belief that you can live a life of positive meaning despite your circumstances can dramatically decrease your painful emotional and physical response to the traumas you've experienced. Although trauma and states of hyper-arousal can disrupt the body's natural equilibrium, becoming aware of your emotional responses can and will have a direct effect on bringing your nervous system back to homeostasis (balance). The emotional power that lies within you is endless!

While our emotional response to life's challenges may leave us feeling helpless, unmotivated, untrusting and reclusive, the irony is that isolation, disconnection and lack of movement make matters worse. Instead, burning off adrenaline and releasing endorphins, exercising and keeping active will help our emotional state tremendously, since it is directly connected to our nervous system. Also, taking time to seek face-to-face support and connection through positive family members, friends, counselors and/or support groups stimulates an emotional and physical pleasure response. This type of energy is powerful.

Additionally, I have found it extremely empowering to attribute *meaning* to my daughter's life and passing. I did this through affirmations like, "We will get through this"; "This will not define us"; "We will make our little part of the world better by expressing our love for our daughter and family out into the world." Through positive statements like these, I created a roadmap for my intentions. Transforming traumas into loving and purposeful intentions brings an amazing depth of meaning to our lives.

Finally, hard as it may be to accept, with intention we can manage every anxious, debilitating and out-of-control feeling we have. By regularly taking time to concentrate on deep breaths filling the diaphragm, we can calm ourselves and transform painful emotions through *mindful breathing*. As you focus on each breath, pay attention to the thoughts, images and sounds that reside in your mind. At first, we might feel like you're in a sea of thoughts, feelings and emotions. Asking questions about the trauma helps you sift through the murky waters.

Notice the answers that surface. You might experience painful feelings of guilt, shame, blame and anger. Take your time and continue to breathe deeply. Do not judge your emotions. Like an investigator, it is your task to be mindful and simply observe. Remember, power lies within you. No one can take it away from you. Each time you go through this breathing exercise, write down in a journal the emotional responses, thoughts, images and sounds that come up. Do not force your emotions to go away. The idea is to observe and become aware of them. The punch and pain of your emotional response to trauma may lessen, as you assign meaning and intention to your life.

Assigning meaning and intention based on your life's traumatic experiences can only take shape through your efforts. But, when you're feeling lost and confused, how can you find meaning in your heartache? I have found that one of the best ways to get meaning and intention back in one's life is by asking powerful "What" questions and eliminating unbearable and futile "Why" questions.

"What" questions like the following will help you create a daily roadmap for your life, the culmination of which will lead you to a life of great meaning and intention:

- What am I committed to in my life *today*?
- What can I do to show my love for my child *today*?

- What can I do to honor my loved one or myself *today*?
- What can I do to improve the world *today*?
- What can I do to honor my body *today*?
- What can I do *today* to help someone who has gone through what I've gone through?

It's important to understand that the emotional pain associated with traumatic circumstances may never entirely leave you, but the hold it has on you most definitely can lessen. Once you wrap your mind around that, you'll have the building blocks to create a meaningful life. I honestly believe you can't expect to feel connected to people and the world around you, until you are first connected with your own internal thoughts and emotions. Once you know how to connect with yourself, connect to others. Keep your body in movement. Engage your nervous system in ways that energize, that calm you and are purposeful. The result will be a life of great meaning and intention.

I now understand that we are all stronger than we know.

My daughter told me so.

Made in the USA
San Bernardino, CA
09 March 2017